GET
YOUR
HANDS

OFF
MY
THROAT

GET YOUR HANDS

by David Wilkerson

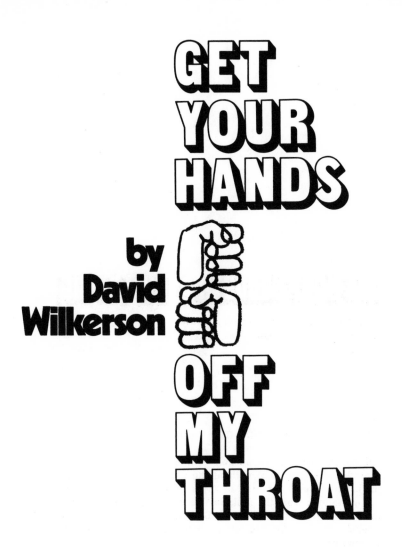

OFF MY THROAT

ZONDERVAN PUBLISHING HOUSE
GRAND RAPIDS, MICHIGAN

Get Your Hands Off My Throat

CONTENTS

I wrote *The Cross and the Switchblade* eight years ago. At that time only ghetto kids were using drugs. Drug addicts told me they had gotten hooked because of alcoholic dads and prostitute mothers. You had to believe them after you saw where and how they lived. Their

INTRODUCTION

excuses for using drugs seemed almost legitimate. Often while ministering in the rat-infested hell of Harlem, I whispered to my heart, "David, you would be a junkie, too, if you had to live like they do."

But now everything has changed. The drug problem affects the whole nation as well as the world. Twelve-year-olds are dying of overdoses. The "goodniks" in suburbia are experimenting with anything to get them up. It's a "stoned" age with a million kids running away from home each year.

Just when we begin to see progress against heroin abuse, a psychedelic revolution hits and kids are caught up with a new drug — then pills, pot, and acid. Now we face the horrible reality of thousands of returning Vietnam veterans hooked on drugs. Jobless, disillusioned, hurt — unable to obtain the powerful strain of M they were accustomed to in Vietnam, they are turning to acid and heroin. Used to violence and handy with firearms, they may be forced by their habits into a life of crime. Already we are taking some of these boys into our treatment centers—hooked and helpless.

Think for a moment of all the young people today who are involved in riots, drugs, rock festivals, and hippie life and who are alienated from parents and God. Think of all those who have walked out on home and the church.

God has been shaking me up recently. It is almost as though His Holy Spirit has taken me by the back of my neck and turned me upside down. This book is the result of hours spent in heart searching about how to reach this generation. I am sharing with you a new look at the drug scene as well as a new look at long hair, rock music, and runaways.

The compassion I felt in writing this book has affected my preaching. One repentant hippie told me recently, "David, the last time I heard you preach, I was turned off. You were hard and made God sound difficult. Tonight you seemed to really care. It wasn't what you said tonight — it was how you said it. Man — I feel love — Jesus love!"

1 Get Your Hands Off My Throat

Get Your Hands Off my Throat

A CALL TO PITY AND PATIENCE FOR THE SPACED-OUT GENERATION

Standing before me was the dirtiest, smelliest hippie I had ever met. His hair was long and probably hadn't been combed in weeks. His worn boots were caked with mud, and months of food stains were permanently pressed into the front of his smelly shirt. His body odor was obnoxious.

When I first saw him, my immediate reaction was, "That is the most irresponsible hippie 'cop-out' I've ever seen. He's a disgrace to society. He's a typical, no-good character who needs to be told how ridiculous he looks."

I put my hand on his shoulder, looked him in the eye, and was just about to lecture him on his looks and manners when he interrupted.

"Mr. Wilkerson, please forgive me for coming to your crusade looking like this. I know I'm dirty and I smell bad. I should have cleaned up, but I just didn't feel like it. When my mother and dad were killed last year, the welfare department put me up in an old flea-bag hotel full of acid freaks and whores. For weeks I just sat on the steps outside feeling lonely and having no friends. I missed my folks pretty badly. One day some kids asked me to turn on with them.

"I had nothing else to do, so I dropped acid. Now every time I get lonely, I turn on. My life is so empty — nothing to live for. Nobody cares. I have no friends. I don't dress like this or wear long hair to be like others. I'm no rebel — I just don't care about anything. But I need help. I need Jesus. I'm desperate. Please don't get hung up about the way I look. Man, please pray for me. Maybe God does love me."

I prayed, all right; and I cried, too. But not just for him. I prayed for myself — that God would forgive me for not showing the pity and patience of Jesus to that lost child. That boy found a new friend in Christ, and this evangelist found a new concept of pity for long-haired, hippie-type kids.

BACKLASH

The worst backlash today is in God's house, among God's people — even in the pulpits of our great churches. It is a backlash against the morals, the wild dress, the abuses, and the lawlessness among our young people. It is a backlash based on the fear that these things will cause us to lose our youth.

This is exemplified by an article in the parish magazine of an English vicar. He wrote, "If the church were to try to communicate successfully today, its buildings would have to be psychedelic pads, its choir girls topless, its hymns bawdy, its prayers replaced by pot and its vicar a well-known pop singer."

But this generation will not be lost to the rebels. Only a small minority of youth have been charmed into revolutionary movements, and rebel leaders are losing their grip. Rebel factions are fighting among themselves and devouring one another. They have been "defanged" by the dollar and spend their time writing memoirs and appearing on TV talk shows.

Radicals rise and fall. Who remembers Rap Brown or Stokely Carmichael — radical Black Panthers who once defied the nation? They are forgotten and powerless.

Black and white rebels will continue to curse God and spit on the flag. They will mock the establishment with four-letter words. Weapons will be stockpiled and cops will be called "pigs." But they will never capture the masses of youth.

John Laslor, a student at Northwestern University, went to Washington, D. C. to march in the moratorium. He waved a Vietcong flag and screamed anti-American slogans at the TV cameras, shaking his fist at the establishment. Returning home, he had second thoughts about what really happened and wrote an article for *Tribune Magazine*. He said.

> My generation may prove to be the biggest pack of hypocrites in history. We've had the most education, the most prolonged childhood, and therefore, the greatest opportunity to think up idealistic theory. Very soon we are going to have to put up or shut up.

Neither will this generation be lost to smut or pornography. The floodgates have been opened; movies are dirty; books are erotic; even television has become smutty. But this baptism of filth has caused a reaction among youth. X-rated movies have become so boring that they no longer draw the big crowds. Teen-agers now prefer conversation, dialogue, and a return to nature.

The Cross and the Switchblade movie, depicting the ministry of the Holy Spirit among gangs and addicts in New York City, played in a twin theater along with a well-publicized, X-rated movie. Thousands attended each night of its two-week premiere in that city; each night was a sellout. In contrast, the X-rated movie played to ten and twelve people a night. The same was true in theaters all over the nation.

Nor am I at all afraid of losing this generation to promiscuous sex. I have been accused of blindness and overstatement, but from where I stand, I see a deepening revolt against the filth pushed on young people by corrupted establishment people.

We will not lose this generation to drugs. There is an increase in drug abuse, but only in small towns and suburban areas. In the hip sections of our major cities there is a trend away from narcotics. Speed is out altogether. LSD is dropping in price and in some areas can hardly be peddled. Marijuana is going out and has become boring to those who are now moving on to "transcendental meditation" and pursuing Eastern religions. Heroin addicts have never been more desperate, and millions of concerned people have rallied to help fight all drug abuse. Parents, schools, local government agencies, churches, and medical groups have launched numerous programs to combat addiction. I repeat — this generation will not be lost to drugs!

PATIENCE

There is only one way to lose this generation. It will not be lost in Haight Ashbury or in East Village, New York. It will not be lost on college campuses or in "shooting galleries" where junkies mainline heroin. It will not be lost as a result of broken homes, broken promises, or a cheating society. If it is to be lost, it will be in unforgiving hearts of parents, officials, and ministers who have lost their pity and patience.

This generation can be doomed and damned by the deaf ears and blind eyes of "Spirit-filled" people who are too steeped in tradition and personal prejudices to understand what is behind the headlines.

We read of riots and campus unrest. Our blood boils when we view scenes of radicals taking over administration buildings with loaded shotguns. Our patriotic spirit is offended and we are deeply hurt by young people who spit on the flag and call cops "pigs." This instinct for decency, law, and order makes us repudiate their acts. We call them Communists and corrupters — and many of them are. We must never be soft on lawbreakers, and we cannot condone their immorality.

Yet, I see a dangerous thing happening in our land today. We are allowing our hurts and fears to drive all compassion from our hearts. We allow our witnessing to turn into warning. Our cries for conformity become more important than our cries for conversion. In our more honest moments we would be forced to admit we would rather see them in jail than at the altar of one of our churches.

How can we reach the radical if we think of him only as a hopeless Communist with no possibility of reform? How can we honestly minister in love to hippies, junkies, and runaways if we see nothing but their clothes and hear nothing but their wrath? How, in the name of mercy, can we reach the hopeless drug addict if we see him only as a sick underachiever who should be locked up to preserve the integrity of society?

Do we write off thousands of black and white college kids who have angered us because of their revolutionary language and violent acts? Do we forsake the multitude of unwashed hippie types because they disagree with our politics or decry the war effort? Even if they were all admitted Communists — even if they hated everything our country stands for — we could not scripturally or morally give up our efforts to reach them with Christ's Gospel. And how can we reach them if we hate them and withdraw?

How can we as Christians minister in love and compassion when we allow our hearts to be overcome with fear and anger? With righteous indignation we demand law and justice. We judge the young generation for its every failure — and not once do we see in them a reflection of our own sins and shortcomings.

After years of preaching Christ in ghettos, I was certain I knew about pity, patience, and compassion. But I had a rude awakening on 103rd Street in Harlem. I had been witnessing to a seventeen-year-old junkie, trying for weeks to reach him, to no avail. One day I lost my composure and, pointing an accusing finger at him, said,

18

"Julio, I've had it with you! You don't want help. You like your junk and you are beyond help. I've wasted enough time on you. You're a big phony." Julio looked surprised. Shaking his head he answered,

"Preacher, I thought you understood, but I see you don't. You just don't know how it is with me. I'm no phony. This is all I know. You've never lived in this neighborhood. I watched junkies shoot heroin when I was six years old. I ran errands for them and cleaned their dirty needles when I was only eight. I grew up thinking heroin was good and a way to forget problems. My mom was a prostitute and my dad was an alcoholic. I lived in the streets. I was sick of life at twelve and wanted to escape from then on. I've been shooting drugs ever since. It's all I know. It's been my life. I thought you understood. You give up too easily. I don't like being a junkie. I just can't get away."

FORGIVENESS

I don't ridicule hippies and long hairs anymore. I'm learning not to be disturbed by their wild clothes or their revolutionary language. I've asked God to let me see beyond all these fronts to hearts that desperately need understanding.

The Bible supports me in a call for a new concept of pity and patience toward young people. Peter asked the Lord how often he was to forgive the trespasser.

> Then Peter approached and said to Him, "Lord, how often shall my brother act amiss toward me and I forgive him? Up to seven times?" Jesus said to him, "I do not say, up to seven, but up to seventy times seven." Matthew 18:21-22.

Christ went on from multiple forgiveness to the concept of pity and patience. To prove His point, Jesus used the parable of a debtor.

> For this reason the kingdom of heaven may be compared to a king who planned to settle accounts with his agents. As he began the settlement, one was brought in who owed him twenty million dollars, but as he had nothing to pay, his master ordered him to be sold, as well as his wife and children and everything he had, and to pay. Then the agent fell down and implored him, "Have patience with me and I will pay you everything." So in pity for that agent his master released him and canceled his debt. Matthew 18:23-27.

This story hits at the heart of the problem in our nation today. Is there anyone among us who cannot identify with this bankrupt man? On the verge of losing everything, he is given a new lease on life through the benevolence, the pity and patience of his master.

Some of us "squares" have forgotten how much we have been forgiven. We seem to have lost sight of what we once were. How much have you and I been forgiven? Let us look into our own hearts and see the horrible things of which we are all capable.

Think back! Was there ever a time in your life when you deserved God's wrath? Did you ever drink excessively, commit adultery or fornication, steal, gamble, kiss another man's wife, smoke habitually? Were you ever guilty of gossiping, backbiting, character accusation, disunity, or some other such secret sin? It is only the pity and mercy of God that saves us! We were rebels and deserved God's wrath and judgment. But He pitied us! He showed us His patience! He forgave!

Ironically, thousands of Christians attend our crusades to rejoice in the story of Christ's redemptive work among the alcoholics, prostitutes, and addicts converted through our TEEN CHALLENGE ministry — only to leave the auditorium and express disgust for long-haired drug users outside the door. We seem capable of loving them once they "prove" themselves worthy or repentant, but we are incapable of loving them while they are in a state of rebellion.

MERCY

> But as that same agent was leaving he met one of his fellow agents, who owed him twenty-five dollars. Grabbing him by the throat, he said, "Pay me what you owe." Then his fellow agent fell down and implored him, "Have patience with me and I will pay." But he refused, and went and threw him into prison until he should pay the debt. Matthew 18:28-30.

The first time I read this account, I was indignant. *What a monster,* I thought. *He is on probation himself, yet he has not an ounce of pity or patience for another. What kind of man is this?*

Now, I hang my head in shame. I am that man. Can you see some of yourself there? How quick we are to demand justice and conformity from others, especially young people. We are so zealous to defend God's holiness — we forget Christ said He would have mercy above the law.

We have been guilty of putting our hands around the throat of underground society and demanding that they conform to our ideas about what to wear and how to act before we will forgive. We forbid them to express their fears and thoughts of rebellion, while we secretly struggle with besetting sins and haunting doubts. Forgetting how patient God has been while we have waded through our doubts about answered prayers, about parents, about God, about life, we expect the young people to shake off all their doubts and stand up yelling, "I believe."

Could it be that this generation is saying to us, "Get your hands off my throat"? Could it be that 400,000 kids wallowed in the mud at Woodstock as if to say, "We are bankrupt. We are in a crisis. We cannot pay up. We just can't conform. Please have patience. Wait a while. Have some pity."

Sure, many of those kids at music festivals sell drugs and lay around in the nude, and I will never condone their actions. But no amount of choking, no amount of pressure, will settle the account. Patience and pity are the only avenues left! They are the only bridges over this gap.

Could it be that thousands of drug users are trying to say, "I'm lost — no identity — I'm searching. I'm unable to cope. Don't push me or choke me. Please be patient. Pity me. Don't give up. I'll pay someday"?

I am stirred to the depths of my soul by these words of Christ:

> Then his master summoned him and said to him: "You contemptible slave! I canceled all that debt for you because you begged me. Should not you have had pity on your fellow servant as I had pity on you?" And angrily his master handed him over to the scourgers, until he should pay everything he owed him. And so will My heavenly Father do to you, if each of you does not heartily forgive his brother. Matthew 18:32-35

God help this generation if the "saints" do not soon learn to forgive and love. Without patience there is no hope left.

We will cast this generation into a prison of eternal despair in the name of justice. The black will hate and be hated. The gaps will become craters — impassable. Hippies and runaways will turn against parents and the church and never return.

Worst of all, the Christian youth who are still marching with us — who are overflowing with love and compassion for their own generation — will see our unforgiving spirit and lack of patience, and they will break away with one voice, "If that is love, if that is the Gospel message, we want no part of it."

Pastor, if you want to reach this generation don't preach to the gallery. Those without pity and compassion may applaud, but teen-agers will turn a deaf ear to all you say. Show them love and patience in your messages. Demonstrate that you care. Forget their clothes and long hair and get to the real issues. Ask God to give you a new baptism of love. Get off their backs and into their needs.

Parents, never give up on them. Be firm and apply discipline — but balance it with patience and pity. Your long-haired children — your hippie-attired teen-agers — have not necessarily gone to the devil. Their rebellion may be only skin deep. If you will be patient, they will come back — frequently all the way.

We can save this generation if we will remember Christ's words:

> Should not you have had pity on (youth) as I had pity on you?

Hair

A LOOK AT PHONY ISSUES

What is the mystique of hair? Those young men who wear it long smile affirmatively at one another as if exchanging a secret code message. Many schools are now abolishing or drastically loosening their dress codes, with expected results: the sloppy kids get sloppier; the neat kids continue to look neat.

Parents and pastors believe it is their personal responsibility to discourage the freaked-out look that is often associated with long hair and wild clothes. But the majority of young people still keep in step with good taste. And long hair appears to be here to stay.

In El Paso, Texas, U.S. District Judge D. W. Suttle ruled that school authorities in that state cannot force young boys to cut their hair as a condition to attending classes. "This country was founded by long-haired people and continues to pay homage to long-haired people." The judge stated that school authorities had failed to show a reasonable basis for denying an education to boys with long hair and giving an education to those with short hair.

THE ESTABLISHMENT ATTITUDE

But many establishment people do not agree with the judge. They are down on longhair, sideburns, and beards. Long-haired prisoners at the Orange County, California, jail are not permitted to work, have recreation hours, or go to worship services if they have shaggy hair and beards. These are weekend prisoners, deprived of TV privileges or visits from ministers. One of the long-haired prisoners said, "Jesus, Himself, couldn't get to church in this jail."

In Reno, Nevada, a judge sentenced nine hippies for littering a park. Their sentence: haircuts.

In one Chicago suburb, police force all long-haired prisoners to get haircuts before they book them and allow them to appear before the judge.

In Hampton, Virginia, a sixteen-year-old boy was brought to trial on a drunk charge. The judge offered to let him go free if he would just cut his long hair.

In Norwalk, Connecticut, a high school principal visited all of his classrooms, pulled out fifty-three students, and suspended them until they got haircuts.

SYMBOL OF REBELLION?

A few educators and psychologists suggest that long hair has become a symbol of rebellion. Some people go so far as to believe it is all part of a Communist plot, a youth rebellion with long hair as its symbol or badge. They suggest it connotes a declaration of war against parents, against squares, against the war in Vietnam, against tradition and the past.

One father said, "The Beatles started all of this. All the kids want today is to look like the Beatles or the Rolling Stones."

LONG HAIR CONVERTS

But things are changing everywhere. Long hair is gaining converts across the country. The mayor of Chicago shocked everybody by saying, "Look at pictures of Christ and Abe Lincoln and you see them with long hair and wigs."

Democratic Congressman Thomas O'Neal of Massachusetts researched the subject and discovered the following:

> Since the time of Christ, the male species has worn long hair and beards about 90% of the time. The Western world turned to short hair and clean-shaven faces only after the Prussian victory over France. All the great heroes of America have worn long hair. It is nothing for Americans to get alarmed about.

Greg, aged seventeen, says, "Being hairy fits me inside and out. It is consistent with my values and attitudes. It also helps me get along with other people. I learn quite a bit about them just by watching them react to me. I've had a beard ever since I was a freshman in high school. Everyone thinks I'm older because of it — maybe I am, but I sure do have a lot of fun with that, too. I've been labeled everything from Samson to Rasputin. I've been called guerrilla, and Moses. I enjoy it. It's all in people. I love people if they are open and responsive. That's part of being hairy, too."

In a recent conference I asked a group of long-haired visitors to explain why they felt it necessary to grow their hair so long. One fellow had hair flowing down over his shoulders.

"It's no big deal, Mr. Wilkerson," he said. "About five years ago when I was seeking God and knew nothing about Him, I went to a movie. I think it was called The Exodus. In it Moses had long hair. So I began to wear long hair because it was the only way I knew how to identify with something religious. I thought it would help me get closer to God."

None of the ten boys I questioned told me they wore their hair long because of any kind of rebellion. Instead, they suggested it was a way of identifying with the old and simple way of life.

THE LANGUAGE OF HAIR

"I wear long hair as a way of telling the world I am my own boss. I want to be like my friends. I want to identify with what's happening and to tell the squares to get off my back. I just simply want to be different."

In recent interviews with other long-haired boys I was told it was their way to shock some sense into people who don't practice what they preach: the drug experts who curse marijuana while getting smashed on whiskey; parents who cry about the moral decay among young people, while they go on with their adultery, fornication and divorce, their mad race for fancy clothes, jewelry, big homes, powerful cars, and material things; self-righteous people who fight against smut and pornography but who think nothing of calling black men "niggers." They suggested that what they really were trying to say was: "You adults had better clean up your own houses before you try to clean up the young people. Get the logs out of your own eyes before you try to remove the little dirt specks from ours."

FROM DUCKTAILS TO SKIN HEADS

Hair styles and fashions change so fast it is impossible to keep up with them. In the early 1950's most of the kids wore crew cuts called "flat tops." In the late 1950's it was the "ducktail," made popular by Elvis Presley. In the late 1960's long hair, sideburns, and beards began to appear. But even while long hair was becoming popular around the world, in London, England, the "skin heads" began to appear as bald as eagles and having a violent spirit of rebellion.

Actually, fashion has become the language of the soul. Young people now define themselves by the way they dress.

I CONFESS

Now, let me make a confession. I used to inwardly despise long hair and wild dress. I loved the young people themselves, but I was deeply upset by the way they looked. I went so far as to coin a term for boys who looked halfway between a she and a him. I called them "shims." A lot of people laughed and many congratulated me for taking such a stand.

One night after I had preached about the "shims," a long-haired, hippie-type boy approached me in the counseling room. I was dressed in a blue blazer jacket with gold buttons, brown and white flare trousers, a striped shirt, and a beautiful wide tie. My shoes were the very latest style. The young man ran his finger up my lapel, looked me right in the eye, and said, "Mister, I can't see Jesus; your clothes are in the way."

I went back to my room and took a hard, honest look at myself and my preaching. I remembered that just five years prior to this time, I had suggested from the pulpit that only effeminate men wore colored shirts. Those were the days when only a few men wore them and it was "proper" to wear only white. Now, many ministers (myself included) are sporting brilliant-colored shirts, wide ties, and flared trousers. Little by little the fashions have been changing, and we have slowly been absorbing them.

Quite accidentally that night I picked up a book which contained pictures of some of the early founders of the Pentecostal movement. I was shocked to see that some of them had beards and mustaches, and a few even had hair halfway down to their shoulders. Also, it suddenly dawned on me that for years I had been looking at Sallman's famous painting of Christ and had never once been chagrined by the fact that he pictured Christ with a long beard and hair flowing down over His shoulders. To me it was beautiful.

THE BIBLE AND LONG HAIR

I decided to spend as much of that night as possible researching everything the Bible had to say about long hair, beards, and dress.

I discovered that God instituted a law in Moses' day against the trimming of beards.

> Do not clip the corners of the hair on your head, nor cut the edge of your beard. Leviticus 19:27

Aaron wore a beard.

> It is like the precious oil upon the head, flowing down upon the beard, Aaron's beard, flowing down upon the edge of his garments. Psalm 133:2

The prophet Ezra had a beard, which he often plucked when he was going through a state of repentance. It was, in fact, a shame in David's time not to have a full-grown beard. David once sent a delegation of ambassadors to King Hanun; the king humiliated them by cutting off one-half of their beards.

> When it was told David, he sent to meet them, because the men were greatly humiliated. The king directed them, "Stay in Jericho until your beards grow out."
> II Samuel 10:5

Long hair was beautiful in King David's time. It was even worth money in the case of Absalom, his son:

> Throughout Israel there was not a man so much to be praised for his looks as was Absalom . . . . When he cut his hair, which he did at the end of every year because it became too heavy for him and he had to cut it, the hair of his head weighed over three pounds, according to the royal standards. II Samuel 14:25-26

THE REAL ISSUE

As I read these Scriptures the Holy Spirit began to deal with me about my approach to the subject of hair and fashions among young people. The Bible says that the Lord does not see as a man sees because man looks on the outward appearance, but God looks on the heart.

We will only isolate young people if we do nothing but scream out against their long hair and wild fashions. These are not the issues. God makes it clear that we are to warn young people to keep their hearts with all diligence, for out of the heart come the true issues of life. God is not interested in the beads and the bell-bottoms. He is interested in the heart.

The Bible warns us that we are not to "judge superficially, but judge fairly" (John 7:24).

If long hair and wild clothes are worn as an act of defiance or rebellion against parents and society, we must judge it as sin — sin which must be rebuked. But at the same time, we must keep in mind that the battle today is not against fashions and fads but against spiritual wickedness.

SPLITTING OVER HAIR

Am I suggesting that ministers and parents delete any reference to long hair and fashions from their conversation and preaching? Absolutely not.

What I am trying to say is that we will only isolate young people if we spend all our time screaming out against what they are doing. It only adds to the subtle thrill and mystique of being different.

It is enough if we can, in love, warn our young people not to be conformed to this world or to wear these styles just to be like others.

We can save this generation if we lead our young people into an act of "body consecration." There needs to be more emphasis on the fact that the body is the temple of the Holy Spirit and cannot be neglected, abused, or made into a spectacle.

A minister came to me recently who was upset by the fact that his seventeen-year-old son was wearing long hair.

He told me, "I just don't like it. A lot of my church members are upset by it, and I think he owes it to me to set a standard for other young people. We've been alienated by this situation, and we are hardly able to talk to one another now."

I talked to the boy later and was convinced he really loved his father. He was certainly not a rebel and he testified to his deep love for Jesus Christ and that he hoped someday to enter the ministry.

When I asked him why the long hair, he answered, "I don't think I should have to carry the load my father is placing on me. I want to be just like any other kid in the church. I personally like a full head of hair, and I don't think it is excessively long. I think if my dad had just left me alone, I would have cut it, but now I have this strange thing about wearing it just because it bugs him so badly. I love him very much, and he's a good man, but he should get off my back."

When the father asked the next day what he should do about his son, I told him he should go directly to the boy and make sure it was no longer an issue. I showed him how tragic it was that he should be alienated from his son just because they disagreed on the length of hair. I also warned him that he was on the verge of losing the boy, not only to himself, but to the cause of God, by his own stubbornness. The father's rigid stand against long hair was a phony issue.

I saw the boy at a youth conference a few weeks later. He still had a full head of hair, but he had cut it halfway. He was neat and well-groomed.

He cornered me after the meeting and said with a smile, "I wish you hadn't talked to my dad. He told me I could wear my hair just as long as I wanted — just so I kept on with Jesus. He asked me to forgive him and said that from now on it was all my decision — the length I was going to wear it. He put all the responsibility on me, and it shook me up. How can you hurt a guy like that? When it was all his responsibility, it was easy. But now that it is my decision, I wound up in the barber shop. Now that dad's losing some hair, mom thinks he should grow his sideburns longer. I think we are going to get along okay now. Thanks, anyhow."

In dealing with young people in my crusades across the country, I have seen the tragic result of ministers and parents who have alienated children by their rigidness concerning fashions. I have met many sons and daughters who have turned against their parents — some with terrible bitterness — because of standards of dress that were forced upon them. I think parents should first set a good example by their own modest dress standards but be sympathetic toward pressures upon young people in regard to the changing styles and fads.

I will never forget the sixteen-year-old minister's daughter who came to me weeping and broken-hearted over the bitterness she held in her heart against her father who pastored one of the largest churches in the city. She had moved into an apartment with a girl friend because she was always fighting with her dad over the length of her skirts or her use of make-up. She walked out the day he told her she could cause him to lose his parish by getting the church people mad over the way she dressed.

The Holy Spirit had convicted her during my preaching and now she sat in the counseling room wanting to be reconciled to her father and to Christ. In broken sentences she sobbed:

"Before I came to this meeting tonight I actually hated my father. I know he's a good man, and God is with him, but he just never did understand what was going on inside of me.

"My parents were always so strict with me that when I got to be fifteen I wanted my independence. I couldn't wear make-up, and my dresses had to be a certain length. Looking back, I know my spirit wasn't right, but if they had only quit harping on the idea that I was grieving God, upsetting them, and ruining their ministry . . .

"I used to sit in church and paint my face while dad was preaching just to bug him. I would wear the shortest dresses I could find and parade up and down the aisles in front of the church people; I got a secret thrill out of watching them stare at me. I wanted to make them all mad. What I wore didn't matter anymore; the only thing that mattered was how independent it made me feel.

"I guess I was trying to tell my father that it was my life and I could live it the way I pleased. What really hurt was that my father just got rigid over it all, and we couldn't communicate anymore. That's when I left home.

"I feel so broken up about it now. It all seems so stupid. I know we were both wrong now, and I just hope he'll understand. I do love him."

There was a wonderful family reunion that night. A teen-age girl who had been alienated from her father was back in his arms crying out all her hurt. And one minister father was bowing his head to ask God for a new spirit of grace and understanding.

Let's take the mystique and the need for rebellion out of long hair and wild fashions. Let's place the burden of responsibility on how to dress with the young people themselves. Let's have enough faith in our young people to believe that once they are filled with Christ and walking in the Spirit, they will make the right decisions about holy living and modest dress. Let's get off their backs and into their hearts!

3 Moses and Music Festivals

Moses and Music Festivals

A PRACTICAL APPROACH TO
NEW MUSIC TRENDS

The Woodstock Music Festival was where many young people claimed they "put it all together." Some 400,000 kids who dressed alike and talked alike and who liked the same kind of hard music and used the same kind of drugs all came together to "do their thing."

Since Woodstock there have been 1,200 other music festivals across the country—some large, some small — but the same kind of people came to do the same kind of thing.

I attended the Laguna Canyon Festival at Laguna, California, where about 20,000 kids jammed into a canyon on Christmas and stayed four days to "celebrate the birthday of Jesus." On stage was erected a white cross and a large statue of the Virgin Mary.

The hillsides were covered with makeshift tents. Thousands sat and slept on the ground on dirty blankets trampled into the mud. Bottles of cheap wine were handed from boy to girl. Marijuana joints were passed around little circles of kids who did nothing but stare into space. Others were selling acid.

One of the festival leaders yelled into the mike, "I hope you're smoking it. That's what it's all about!"

In little tents couples were engaging in sexual acts. The foul smells and dirty surroundings made it all seem so cheap.

The food line was pitiful. There were no dishes and few utensils. Kids grabbed a piece of cardboard or an old tin can. Beans and salad were dumped on these dirty containers to keep unwashed, hungry young people from starving.

The crowd was stoned. I couldn't find ten kids who weren't smoking pot. Many were on bad acid trips and were being carried to the medical tent. Although this was supposed to be a festival to celebrate the birth of Jesus Christ, the participants were so high they didn't even remember it was Christmas.

WHY THE FESTIVALS?

It took about an hour before the full impact hit me! Everywhere I saw wild hair, wild clothes, wild music, wild drugs, wild dancing! Tears fell freely.

I prayed, "Oh, God, why are they here? Why do they eat and sleep and live like animals? Why do they flaunt the marijuana and acid and pills so openly? Why do they sit for days in the mud and cold on freezing mornings and damp nights? What power is behind it all? What's happening? Is it all a bad dream that will pass? Where are the parents? Who missed these children? Can we reach them? Is it too late?"

I have spent the past twelve years combatting all kinds of drugs and fighting for the souls of addicts. Everybody knows where I stand on dropouts, speed freaks, and uncommitted rebels. *But* — I think it is time to listen to what this new generation is saying — it is time to open our hearts to them.

That is the only reason I climbed on a Honda cycle and went to the Laguna Festival. I went there to listen. And I got it from all sides:

> "The square world is one of cocktail parties. They drink whiskey like water, cheat on taxes, climb those social ladders, and tramp people down in the process — and call it success."

> "Parents think nothing of getting a divorce and messing up the lives of all the kids. Teachers and cops go on strike and curse the bosses. Adults declare the wars and make us kids go fight them. They hide under white sheets and burn crosses . . . cheat on wives and husbands and put on a big front like they are really in love."

> "You hate our long hair, but you wallow in wigs. You put us down for funny looking clothes; then your fashion designers steal the look and make it popular the very next year.

You mocked our granny glasses, and now you wear them."

"You spend millions to build big churches. You put a man upfront who doesn't like God — doesn't believe the Bible — and then you condemn us for seeking comfort and religious feelings with LSD and pot!"

"Your baldheaded men make the dirty movies and produce the smut, and you condemn us for looking at it. You provide us with birth control pills and cry out about our morals. You entice us everywhere we turn with sexy ads — then put us down for going all the way at a drive-in movie."

I went home that night and began to search my Bible. I found some real answers! About festivals! About how to reach those who attend!

THE FIRST FESTIVAL

The world's first and biggest music festival was held — not by Americans — by the children of Israel. And was it big! Although some 400,000 attended Woodstock, more than 3,000,000 attended the wilderness celebration.

To understand the festival phenomenon of our day, we must go back to Moses and the wilderness festival. The story is almost incredible, but it is true. And it traces clearly the downward steps of Israel which finally ended in a wild, devilish, musical debauchery.

Suggesting that rock music can be a quasi-religious force, Professor Benjamin DeMott of Amherst said, "It leads me past myself, beyond myself, beyond my separateness and difference into a world of continuous blinding sameness — and, for a bit, it stoneth me out of my mind."

STONED ON ROCK

I think the professor hit the nail on the head. It was this overwhelming desire to "get stoned" that led to the first music festival in the wilderness. Moses was on the mountain, with God. He left behind him a nation that had been visited by God like none other in all history. The elders and religious leaders had eaten in God's presence; God had revealed His power and glory in a fiery demonstration on top of the mountain. They had heard an audible promise of protection, success, and divine blessing.

Yet in about forty days time, in the absence of Moses, a spirit of lust, a spirit of doubt, and a spirit of rebellion had engrossed the nation. How quickly they turned away from tradition, from their promises, from their spiritual heritage.

See them dancing in the nude around an idol of materialism. Witness the tragic downfall of the ministry in the compromising Aaron. All he can offer as an excuse is that "I am only giving them what they ask for — only adjusting myself to the taste of the crowd."

Combine a lust for pleasure, a capacity for doubt, and a compromising ministry, and you have the recipe for a national moral landslide.

I ask you—where were the fathers of Israel? Where were the deacons, the elders, the judges, and the mothers of Zion? Did they all capitulate to the overpowering zeal and recklessness of younger people? Why is there no record of one committee, one family, one person standing before that festival crowd gone berserk to cry out: "This is wrong; it's rebellion. We have been hypnotized by some strange and powerful trend — awake — turn to Jehovah God!"

DECIBELS AND DEBAUCHERY

God cut short His visit with Moses and commanded him to return to his people.

> The Lord said to Moses: Go, get down, for your people, whom you brought up from the land of Egypt have behaved wickedly. They have quickly swerved from the path in which I directed them; they have made for themselves a molten calf, have sacrificed to it and have said, "This is your god, O Israel, who brought you up from the land of Egypt." Exodus 32:7-8

How quickly they corrupted themselves! How quickly they developed strange tastes! How quickly they turned from the old paths! How quickly they changed from those who trembled at God's glory to those who evidently saw no wrong in dancing nude before a golden calf! How true God's Word — men shall become "lovers of pleasure rather than lovers of God."

What a shocking sight for Moses as he came upon the scene. I think he found it impossible to believe things could change so fast. He couldn't recognize his own people.

> And when Joshua heard the noise of the people as they shouted, he said unto Moses, There is a noise of war in the camp. And he said, It is not the voice of

them that shout for mastery, neither is it the voice of them that cry for being overcome: but the noise of them that sing do I hear. Exodus 32:17,18,KJV

There was singing — but to the ears of Moses it was nothing but noise! Decibels of debauchery!

Everything that happens at music festivals today happened there! They even brought peace offerings. Nothing is really new! If the sounds we hear today are performed by people in a state of rebellion, and if those sounds originate from a desire to rise up and play — if they lead to sexual immorality and moral abandonment — if they promote idolatry of any kind, then they are nothing but noise!

THE BEGINNING OF PROTEST MUSIC

We are in the midst of an electrical explosion of sound. Sensory overloads have been developed by music manipulators as a means of liberating the self, expanding consciousness, and rediscovering the universe. Rock sounds of the early 60's are now electronically magnified by synthesizers like the "Moog" and the "Byrd-Durreth." The appetite of rock producers and musicians to take young minds back into the world of medievalism and tribalism has become so obsessive that recording studios now have to install twenty-four-track tape machines to reproduce sounds.

We are in a period of protest sounds — music so complex and frenzied it takes on an image of soul language. Music is now a vehicle used to by-pass tradition, and rock groups and rock music represent a total way of life influencing hair styles, wardrobe, revolution, drugs, parents, sex, language, war — and anything that has to do with discovering a new way of life.

The vibrating colors, blinding images, deafening sounds, swirling bodies, and spaced-out minds have become a launching pad for teen-agers into the "hip" world.

Rock has become a renaissance of hostility. Young people appear tough, restless, frustrated, aggressive, defiant, alienated — and their music reflects their innermost feelings.

Psychedelic music has an electronic, elemental, pounding beat of primitiveness. It demands the whole person and becomes a "soul" experience. The youth who are caught up in it seem to be saying to society: "This sound moves something in the deep of me — a kind of feeling — a spirit thing — something parents can't tell you about or experience."

RELIGION AND ROCK

But the protest music of this generation is more than just rebellion against the establishment and "over-thirty" values. It is more than a protest against materialism, hypocrisy, and phoniness. Rock has been called "the most important music of all time" *(Life)* — and its importance, as I see it, has to do with the spirit force behind it.

I stood for three hours in the middle of the Electric Circus in East Village, New York, trying to understand and relate to more than a thousand young people swirling to the deafening roar that shook the building. The words were totally unintelligible, the performers were so stoned they couldn't possibly know what they were playing on their instruments, but it was loud

— electronically beefed up — and it so overloaded the senses that young people were overwhelmed by decibels.

Not a word passed between the dancers, but a language was being spoken, loud and clear. It seemed to me their spaced-out bodies were saying, "I understand what is happening — I feel it too. It's mystical; it's deep; it touches something in me that seeks freedom; it uncages the pent-up me."

For those who refuse to experiment with drugs, acid rock music is a substitute high. It creates an atmosphere of adventure and a way to unleash the mind from the boundaries that have prevailed for centuries. You can now blow your mind on sound — the Detroit sound, the Nashville sound, the Memphis sound, or the Chicago sound. It comes in all shades of acid — rockabilly, baroque, raga rock, bluegrass rock, soul rock, aleatory rock, and studio rock.

Rock is invading even the sanctuaries of the most traditional churches. In Elizabeth, New Jersey, a Roman Catholic priest serves as the lead singer of the Heart Beats, a rock group from the Sacred Heart High School. In the spring of 1968 the Electric Prunes rock group recorded *Mass in F Minor*. And while some evangelical churches condemn this "Holy Ghost" rock, they allow gospel quartets to stomp out their rockabilly beat which closely resembles acid rock.

Now I'm not planning to launch into a tirade against Christian rock groups or the strange new music forms in the church. But I am interested in ways to reach the festival crowd — those stoned, rebellious, alienated young people who sit at the Woodstocks and the Lagunas absorbing this music, looking for a purpose to exist.

What kind of a man was Moses, who could stand in the midst of this immoral, frenzied festival and have his heart broken with compassion? God was ready to destroy these corrupted people; He was grieved because they were stiff-necked and rebellious and deserved the full impact of heaven's judgment.

But Moses stood before God and offered his own life in exchange for mercy on their behalf.

> . . . this people has sinned an enormous sin; they have made for themselves a god of gold. And yet if Thou wilt forgive their sin . . . and if not, please blot me out of Thy book which Thou hast written. Exodus 32:31,32

How unlike me — how unlike you! We look with disdain on these "long-haired rebels" who float from one festival to another. We call them: Irresponsible! Hopeless! Junkies! Dirty bums! Sex maniacs!

Oh, God, give us the spirit of Moses. Sure, this generation deserves the wrath of God. Certainly they are stiff-necked and rebellious! But someone is needed to withstand the wrath of God with compassionate prayer and intercession. These kids are the sons and daughters of parents just like you and me. They were once tender, innocent children who romped and played with mothers and dads — who once had goals and dreams — now gone forever.

God helping me, I will never again condemn them from my pulpit. I will not look down on them as ragged rebels. I see them now as a generation caught up in a world-wide spirit of immorality — a generation that needs a Savior. I see them as Moses saw his children — individual souls worth saving.

Yet love is never blind. Compassion never covers up sin. No sooner had Moses withstood God's wrath than he suddenly stood at the gate of the camp and called for a separation. He stopped the music. He drew a line and demanded that every person make a choice.

> Moses stationed himself at the camp entrance and said, "To me, whoever sides with the Lord!" All the Levites then joined him. Exodus 32:26

This must be our message to the festival crowd of our day. "Get on one side or the other." Those who preferred nudity, sensuality, and idolatry were told to stay, confirmed in their sins. Those who wanted God — those who wanted to come back — were to cross the line.

To every festival goer I say, "You can't have Christ and pot too! Drop your drugs, reject your phony friends. Come out and separate yourself. Take your stand now!"

In youth crusades across the country I am preaching with wet eyes and a newly broken heart. But my message is clear — separate! Come back! All the way!

I cannot close this chapter without sharing my feelings about the new rock sounds now heard so frequently in religious circles.

Christian rock groups are brought to our youth crusades by sponsoring churches. They appear on my stage with their drums and loud guitars, handclapping their way through songs that speak of Jesus, but with the primitive beat borrowed from the Beatles or some other hard rock group. I try not to act surprised, offended, or ashamed. You see, I want so much to relate to these young people.

The kids in the audience seem to love every beat.

They clap, they smile, they relate, they turn on, and they get excited. But something inside me, deep in my soul, does not feel right. There's a small hurt which I can't suppress; I feel uneasy. Somehow I am grieved, and I can't explain it. I feel as though the Holy Spirit within me does not witness to the rock sounds in the middle of a salvation meeting. I also have a sense, an inner knowledge, that the gentle Holy Spirit is not comfortable in the atmosphere this music creates.

At first I tell myself it is only me — my "over-thirty" taste dictating caution. I recall all the arguments I've heard recently about why this kind of music is relevant and acceptable. I am told that kids have developed a different taste in music than my generation had. They think of it as their very own music, a part of their world. Old methods and music styles are no longer reaching them — so I am told.

Modern composers keep warning me that I'd better "get with it" or be left out; that I'll never reach teenagers if I condemn their music or refuse to allow rock type music in my crusades. Then, too, ministers tell me they don't really like the new music trend, but they bring in Holy Ghost rock groups because it "packs the kids in."

For the past two years I have fought a battle in my soul that I believe many other ministers are fighting also — how far shall I go regarding the new rock sound? Is religious rock just a passing fad? Is it really harmful, or am I too cautious? Or is there some hidden danger of which I am not aware? If I condone rock music, will these young people to whom I minister also develop an appetite for all the things that are usually associated with it — the wild fashions, the drugs, the rebellion, and the rejection of our society?

I have tried to be brutally honest with myself on this matter. For instance, what about the old-time revival meeting days when people strummed on banjos, clapped their hands, and danced "Jericho marches" to the militant music of that era? What about the Gospel quartet concerts where the "saints" gather to witness the gospel spectaculars which feature the liveliest beat this side of Elvis Presley? If I condemn rock music, I'll have to honestly condemn all of the primitive beat music, from camp meetings to Gospel quartets. If I am to suggest that young people smash their rock records, I must also ask them to smash many of the Gospel records which borrow the same beat.

I can't condemn the performers, either. Some of the religious rock musicians are dedicated Christians. In spite of their styles and mannerisms, I have seen many of them conducting prayer sessions, prior to their performance, begging God to bless their efforts. Apparently they meant every word of it.

What is the answer for me as a parent and as a minister? I want to speak to this problem with real compassion and concern — and yet I want to be sure I will never offend the Holy Spirit. I can only speak as one man, as one who seeks answers to modern youth problems.

I must honestly admit that I don't like rock music in any religious meeting. In fact, I don't like rock music at all. But I cannot condemn the composers who write it, the people who perform it, or the young people who have developed a taste for it. Rather, I want to suggest some practical and scriptural guidelines regarding all music. All music in the name of Jesus Christ or the church must measure up to the Word of God. I suggest three simple guidelines.

1. MUSIC CAN BE LOUD — BUT NEVER LEWD.

Sing joyfully to God our strength; Shout for joy to
Jacob's God. Psalm 81:1

Loudness never offends God — lewdness does. It is
lewd to wiggle, squirm, and prance in costumes de-
signed to do nothing more than bring attention to the
body. It is lewd to override a good musical message
with a beat so frenzied it becomes evident the performers only want to excite or "grab" an audience. It
is lewd to sing only for applause. It is lewd to use the
name of Jesus to promote a personal taste in music or
in an effort to get others to accept a certain trend. It is
lewd to sing or perform in any new style just to prove
that you are really "with it." It is lewd to relate to the
crowd rather than to Jesus. It is a repetition of Aaron's
sin to offer the crowd what they demand rather than
to set good standards in taste and style.

2. MUSIC CAN BE JOYFUL — BUT NEVER JESTING.

Nor should there be indecency and foolish talking or
low jesting; they are not fitting. Instead, let there
rather be thanksgiving. Ephesians 5:4

The Bible encourages the clapping of hands and
joyful sounds. Jubilant music belongs to victorious
Christians — it is their trademark. But there is a kind
of music which represents jest. It is nothing but a joke.
The performers are not "giving thanks" for victories
won or blessings received. Instead, they sing out their
own frustrations because they are still clinging to old
habits and unholy secret living. They go to the sanc-
tuary to perform as jesters in God's holy court.

Spiritual songs and joyful music speaks to the heart, not the muscles. When the music results in nothing but muscle twinges, seat squirming, and surface feelings, it is jest. If the outcome of this joyful sound is the praising of God, it is good and uplifting. But if it leads to foolish talking, if it promotes a mood of frolic and fun, it is nothing but jest.

The only purpose of Christian music should be to move the hearts of men closer to God.

3. THE MUSIC MUST NEVER OVERSHADOW THE MESSAGE.

Speaking one to the other in psalms and hymns and spiritual songs, singing heartily and making your music to the Lord. Ephesians 5:19

The newest and most uplifting trends in Gospel music today can be found among the new Jesus people on the West Coast. They gather in circles and quietly sing their lilting music of psalms put to melody. It is beautiful and scriptural and has a life-giving message.

Compare that with some of the sounds to which we are exposed today — loud, torrid background music behind a soloist or vocal group who scream unintelligible words into a high-powered microphone. Probably some of the religious rock groups are singing beautiful words, but who will ever know? Turn down the background and maybe we'll get the message.

I believe the key to all Christian music can be found in Ephesians 5:19 — spiritual songs. We are to sing psalms and hymns to each other. It is fine to set these great messages to modern melodies, but let us be sure the spiritual message is not overpowered by the primitive beat of the beast in us.

Music styles will keep on changing. The festivals may pass from the scene completely. A new sound might soon arise which will be far more primitive and frenzied than rock music. But one thing will remain constant — the heart that is filled completely with love for Jesus Christ will never knowingly grieve the Holy Spirit with unChristlike music, styles, or conversation. The heart truly filled with the Spirit will be led into the beautiful praises of God and will never develop an appetite for music that is loved and promoted by unChristlike individuals.

4 The Jesus Revolution

THE GOOD AND THE BAD

There were about five hundred of them — hippies of all kinds. Long-haired, bare-footed girls draped in shawls and sporting granny glasses. One fellow wore earrings and a huge lady's hat topped off with a flower spray and a big green feather.

Perhaps ten had guitars with them, and most carried Bibles. They were all part of the crowd at our Northwest crusade. Thousands of copies of my book, *The Cross and the Switchblade,* had been distributed free on the streets and in the public schools. It looked to me like every hippie type in the city had come to our meeting. They sat on the floor, in the aisles, on the steps, and many of them were stretched out, using guitars and jackets for headrests.

Addicts, prostitutes, alcoholics, or hippies — none turn me off — God has called me to reach them all for Christ. I've worked with all types on the streets, in crusades, and at TEEN CHALLENGE. But this night I felt something strange. Ushers were baffled as they stepped over hippies to pass the offering baskets. A few ministers were worried that they might try to take over the meeting or get violent. But that was not what bothered me. I felt something in the deepest reach of my soul, almost sinister and overwhelming.

God, help me judge fairly. God, help me see beyond beards, bell-bottoms, and long hair. May I never be rude or sarcastic about the way kids dress or behave. Help me to show pity and patience to young people who are hooked and in despair through drugs, broken homes, and loneliness. But, dear God — don't let me be blind to the devices of Satan as he goes about as a roaring lion to devour and deceive young people.

More than 6,000 people filled the auditorium that night, the majority under twenty-one. As I preached, the hippies yelled, "Right on, Davie. Right on." They were a kind of modern-day amen corner urging me to give it all I had. If I made a good point, some would hold their Bibles overhead and cry, "It's all in the Book." Their interruptions didn't bother me a bit, but even though I couldn't put my finger on it, in my heart I had an ever-growing sense that these "hippie Christians" did not completely witness to my spirit.

They called themselves "The Jesus People," and when I gave the invitation they swarmed forward and into the counseling rooms. In all my crusades I have prayer circles in the counseling rooms. About fifteen seekers at a time gather around me, and placing their hands on mine, we all "agree together" for a miracle in each life. Hundreds of young people are helped each night in these "Jesus circles." But the prayer circles this night proved to be quite different. While moving from one circle to another, I was suddenly surrounded by my first hippie group. All around me, with hands joined in the middle, were about fifteen of the "Jesus people" — the hippie Christians. Others were standing in their own circle. The deep circles under the eyes, the washed-out look, the far-off gaze, and the frail bodies meant only one thing to me — they had been using narcotics.

One young man spoke up, "Mr. Wilkerson, we're the Jesus people. We came to pray for you and help you counsel other kids."

One of them prayed — sincerely, honestly, and directly. *Was I wrong? Had I misjudged them?* These and other thoughts raced through my mind. *Could it be God is doing some new thing and taking the church out into the open air, to communes, to the city parks, to music festivals? Could it be the Holy Spirit has been outpoured on these hippies and they are new "evangelists" to this generation?*

I have been predicting for years that a spiritual awakening is coming to youth and that it will be the greatest in all history. Perhaps these hippie Christians represented a vanguard for a new, revolutionary church that would reach this generation for Christ! Maybe this was the breakthrough.

They told me about their street meetings, about distributing literature, about forsaking all to preach Jesus. Maybe this was the beginning of the Jesus revolution we had been expecting.

Yet I still could not quiet my spirit. I loved these young people and wanted more than anything else in the world to understand them. I had no desire to make them conform in any way.

I prayed silently that the Holy Spirit would show me why I felt so uneasy — and it did not take long for the answer to come. One of their young ladies sidled up to me and began to pour out a torrent of their philosophy and ideas.

A JESUS TRIP

According to them, Christ was a "cool cat," they were all "zapped" by the Holy Spirit, and they had added Jesus to their "bag." They talked about Jesus as if He were a super acid trip — a "way out" experience that could make you really high. They spoke of Jesus in such glowing terms, and love was everything. They were really turned on to Jesus and wanted everybody else to "trip out" on Him too. Others joined in and told me how it was. "Wow, man, Jesus is for real. Like wow — He's really heavy. Like, man, wow, it's the thing. Jesus, wow, man, I dig Him. Wow, like I mean He's the ultimate trip. Like, wow, man, Jesus really puts you up, like wow!"

Was it just their way of explaining the realities of Jesus as they saw it? I looked the young man right in the eye and asked, "Now that you're spaced-out on

Jesus, what about your drugs? How about all the free love stuff? How about pot and acid?"

With a little hurt in his voice, he answered, "But you don't seem to understand. Pot is groovy. You can meet the Lord through acid. There's nothing wrong with these things God made for us — just so Jesus is first. We've added Jesus, and it's wonderful."

The pieces started to fall into place. Here were a group of young people who claimed to be Jesus people, an army of Jesus revolutionaries, who had not been to the Cross. They knew nothing of being sanctified, of holy living, of separation from the world and old habits and immoral friends. Jesus was a bigger, better trip in a series of trips and experiences.

Please don't get me wrong. Not all of these hippie "Christians" were still using drugs and indulging in free love and permissive sex. Some were beginning to reach out in faith, and counselors were showing them from the Scriptures that crucifixion of the old nature has to be. Those who were being reached would leave the crusade and turn away from all drugs; they would become genuine Jesus people.

But it hurt to realize many of them would pick up their guitars and Bibles and go on their way singing "Jesus songs" — still bound, still hooked, still full of self — down on the church, down on society, down on parents, down on the government, with eyes full of adultery and fornication! They would still conduct their prayer meetings where "under the spirit" they would strip off their clothes and dance in the nude. They would smoke pot to "make Jesus more real" and drop acid to make the Bible come alive. They would continue to use the name of Jesus freely, and they would do many great works in His name — while still continuing in their evil ways.

THE JESUS CRY

Their coming is predicted in the Word of God. We are clearly warned that "phonies" will appear and attempt to infiltrate the kingdom of God. They will be distinguished by their cry of "Jesus, Jesus!"

> Similarly you will know people by the deeds they do. Not everyone who says to Me, "Lord, Lord!" will enter into the kingdom of heaven, but he who does the will of My Father in heaven. Many will say to Me on that Day, "Lord, Lord, did we not prophesy in Your name and in Your name cast out demons and in Your name do many wonderful works?" Then I will frankly say to them, "I never knew you. Get away from Me, you evil workers." Matthew 7:20-23

I believe this passage refers to some of the new revolutionary "Christians" who call themselves by the Lord's name but who still work iniquity. They want their drugs, their free sex, their own way — all this and Jesus too. They prophesy in the Lord's name, they pray over people and expect miracles, they go about doing good and performing wonderful works in the name of Jesus. They operate communes and feeding programs housing the homeless and caring for the needy. But on Judgment Day God will say,

> Depart, I never knew you. You tried a short cut. You used the name of Jesus freely but didn't obey His commandments. You prophesied and preached like a zealous missionary, but all the while you were never regenerated. You still indulge in your old habits and continue to work evil. Depart! I don't know you — I never did know you. You were never a real Jesus person. You only used His name to hide your sins.

I am not judging any particular group, but there are among us now a growing number of deceivers, walking after their own flesh, who promise liberty while they themselves are in bondage.

Satan desires to discredit the real Jesus revolution by promoting a phony one that by-passes the blood of Christ and total commitment to holiness and separation.

JESUS — A NATIONAL PREOCCUPATION

Yet in spite of the "many" who come in Christ's name as deceivers, a deep and honest Jesus revolution has started and is gaining momentum daily. The movement of the Holy Spirit among hippies in Southern California, and now widespread throughout the South and Midwest, is genuine. Look magazine (8 February 1970) focused attention on a "national preoccupation" of young people centered on Jesus. I personally know of the great work God is doing in Los Angeles among hippie types. From Sunset Strip to the beaches at Laguna, thousands of former drug users are surrendering to Christ and cleaning up. I know for a fact these converts are going straight.

Four years ago when I appeared on the Mike Douglas and Art Linkletter shows, I predicted a Jesus revolution. I rejoice to see the evidence all around that this is now happening.

A growing number of the Hell's Angels motorcycle gang have been truly converted and now preach Christ from atop their machines. Music festivals are being invaded by young converts who have been delivered from narcotics and who now do all they can to turn off others through Jesus. Major record companies no longer promote rock groups who use and preach drugs, nor records featuring a drug theme. Even rock singers are turning to Jesus. Many hit songs of recent months have been religious in nature, among them "Oh, Happy Day" and "Amazing Grace."

Bibles are being carried unashamedly by high school and college students on campuses everywhere. There is a tremendous interest in Bible study among students, and small study groups are springing up across the land.

Instead of the peace signs, there are now the Jesus signs. A single finger lifted high stands for one Lord — one way. A thumb to thumb handshake is a secret code which says, "I'm one of the Jesus people." Bumper stickers now read "Jesus loves you" and "Christ is coming soon." Lapel buttons proclaim, "I'm a Jesus person."

Christian underground newspapers have sprung up in many areas. In some places they now outsell the radical underground papers. These papers run full-page advertisements about baptismal services, Bible studies, witnessing crusades, and spiritual events of all kinds.

THE SQUARE REACTION

The Jesus revolution is here, and it has many young people, parents, and ministers confused. In Jacksonville, Florida, a group of Christian young people gathered around me for a rap session about the new hippie Christians. Long-haired, bearded, shoeless, some of these new Christians were walking around the auditorium and through the school corridors trying to turn everybody on to Jesus. They carried big Bibles and a group would "capture" a teen-ager, surround him, and in their own effervescent way tell of their "great big high with Jesus."

The "square" teen-agers who gathered around me were upset. An attractive fifteen-year-old girl spoke up:

"Look at them, Mr. Wilkerson, with their scraggly hair and unwashed clothes, telling us we need more of the love of Jesus. Telling us we take Christ for granted. They come to church barefooted and are promoted in our meetings as some big new deal. So what if they quit drugs; we never started. So what if they want to go off on some joy pop Jesus trip; we don't think Christ is just another trip. What's going on? Why don't they at least comb their hair or wash their clothes? Doesn't serving Jesus mean being responsible too?"

These Christian "straights" were neither angry nor prejudiced; they simply could not understand what they considered contradictions in the lives of certain Jesus people.

One teen-age boy asked, "Do I have to get 'hip'? Do I have to go into, then out of, the drug scene? Do I have to dress like one of them to be a part of the Jesus movement?"

There is growing apprehension among parents and ministers that converted hippie types who still cling to old manners will seduce the "straights" to embrace the hippie way of life. It is unsaid, yet apparent, some kids are thinking, "They had their fling; they dropped acid and smoked pot; they experienced the forbidden things of life and came back. Now they are the front lines. They are more knowledgeable about life. They keep their hippie flair and still have Jesus — maybe I can do it all and come back too!"

Let's set the record straight. A Jesus person walks a Jesus walk.

> He that saith he abideth in him (Jesus) ought himself also to walk, even as he walked. I John 2:6 KJV

In our desperate effort to relate to the spaced-out youth of our generation, we have innocently fallen into a subtle trap set by the enemy. Young people who have been "tripping out" on drugs seek a substitute high. They seek another state of euphoria. They want to "go up" on Jesus. But we must be careful to tell these young people the whole story — about tribulation, suffering, persecution, rejection by the crowd, separation, and valley experiences.

A young acid head came to me recently and confessed: "David, I used to be a fanatic for Jesus. I quit drugs and got high on Jesus. Man, I was really groovin' with the Man — I tripped out on God. But it was a bummer. I'm down, man. It was all a bad scene."

He was back on drugs and tripping on acid worse than before. Like so many in the Jesus movement of today, he tripped with his head but not his heart. He refused to give up the old crowd; he went to the same old places. He changed nothing but his manner of getting high. No wonder it was a "bummer!"

I no longer use terms such as "high" or "trip" to relate any Christian experience. It has to be so much more — a total surrender — a death! Many today are so high on Jesus that they can't settle down. But my Bible says every man is a phony unless he is securely grounded.

Whoever comes to Me and listens to My words and does them, I will show you whom he resembles. He resembles a man who built a house; he dug and went down deep and set the foundation on a rock. When the flood arose, the river rushed against that house but had no power to shake it, because it was securely built. Luke 6:47,48

5 Spaced-Out

Spaced-Out

A NEW AND HONEST APPROACH
TO DRUG ABUSE

Drugs hit! Suddenly the entire community turns into a kind of gigantic PTA. Newspapers run series of shocking articles about drug abuse. Panels are organized; civic groups launch into studies. Investigations are started; crisis centers are opened. Human relations councils mobilize and spend time with students trying to "understand" them. Then the good old school district gets into the fight by adding "drug problems" to its agenda and calls in experts to plan an educational program for assemblies.

Suddenly everybody wants to hear it and tell it "like it is." Overnight schools are bombarded by experts: "expert" doctors, narcotic agents, police chiefs, ex-addicts, even "expert" parents.

All of this results in a media panic and an anti-pot journalism crusade. The newest fad in radio and television programming is the "drug special." The intent of most of this written and televised material on drugs is to scare the daylights out of potential abusers and alarm parents into action.

It's all one big mess! Too many preachers are preaching emotionally against drugs; too many writers are writing inaccurately about drugs; too many singers are singing about drugs; too many well-meaning parents and experts are telling too many half-truths and lies about drugs — and it all winds up with too many young people using drugs. Consequently, many of these kids learn to mistrust adult society and what it says, and they mistrust its attitude toward drugs.

Many students have become polarized by the over-simplifications about drug abuse, such as: "All long hairs are junkies." "The hippie types are just Communists trying to demoralize teen-agers with dope."

The way I look at it, if we'd quit blaming the Communists and the Cosa Nostra for the drug abuse in this country and get to the real causes, we might be able to do something about solving this problem.

THE TRUTH ABOUT DRUG ABUSE

The high school health class movies depict drug users as people who have failed to adjust and develop a normal way of life and are in some way totally inadequate to compete. Drug use is pictured as a sordid, underworld indulgence by sick and desperate people who sit around in smoky, rat-infested rooms. Only the dead-end of drug abuse is shown, with all of its vomiting, its horrible addiction, its heartbreak, its disillusionment, and its culmination in death. Much of the educational material shows the drug user as a bug-eyed freak who is not only dirty and stupid but also a jerk who smokes a few sticks of pot and suddenly becomes a mainline junkie.

Then comes the big shock! A best friend who is on the honor roll and is a three-letter man in sports confesses that he has been smoking pot most of the time. Stories begin circulating that the rich kid from the Ivy League school is turning on with drugs. The rigid stereotype that the poor, the blacks, the artists, and the dropouts are the average drug users suddenly goes up in smoke.

The real truth of the matter is that often the most successful, intelligent, and individualistic students are among those who are turning on with drugs.

Narcotics can induce such tremendous feelings of exhilaration that logic alone cannot restrain young people from trying them over and over again. Even philosophers and well-known celebrities have not been able to defend themselves against the mystique of drug use.

Although its use is considered boring to many, marijuana has become an element of youth culture and has taken a deep root in the soil of this generation's rebellion against society. It cannot be uprooted by lectures, warnings, and threats. Drug use will not diminish as long as those in authority spend all their time dealing with the symptoms rather than getting to the cause.

1. *Availability*

An estimated 300,000 servicemen have returned from Vietnam with drug problems. In the service, drug abuse is a result of boredom, fear, a sense of wasting time, and easy accessibility to drugs. Availability plays a large role in our country, too. It is probable that a young person will not choose to smoke pot if there is none available or if he has never seen anyone else smoking it.

2. *Loss of Normality*

After World War II a whole new series of abnormal procedures was introduced into the American way of life. It was regarded as only temporary, and everybody was convinced we would get back to normal someday. Adults remembered the quiet warm nights, the Fourth of July parades, and the simple pleasures such as swinging on the front porch. Now we face complicated and seemingly unsolvable problems everywhere. Those good old days have never returned; the abnormal is considered normal by many students. To many, rebellion is a way of life. To their parents, pill-popping has become a way of life, and so many students see marijuana evolving as their normal way of life.

3. *The Influence of Rock Groups*

Rock groups turn more kids on to drugs than any other factor today. From center-stage they preach that pot and acid "are a groove." These groups appear in concert where fans finally get a chance to meet musicians who have been their absolute idols. The kids hear dope being glamorized on stage and hear the musicians doing a ten-minute dialogue encouraging and condoning the use of drugs. These groups specifically exploit heroin and other hard drugs. There are many records with veiled or overt endorsements of narcotics of all kinds.

The original purpose was to grab large student audiences and to prove that the musical groups were really with it. But many performers got hooked on stuff just to maintain their images. For some — like Janis Joplin, Jimi Hendrix, and Brian Jones — it meant death. Groups involved in this drug culture include The Loving Spoonful; Jefferson Airplane; The Rolling Stones; Crosby, Stills, Nash and Young; and the Beatles.

4. Loneliness

In this day of unparalleled affluence, loneliness is eating at the vitals of young people. One seventeen-year-old addict expressed her loneliness like this:

> I wanted to be an ostrich —
> To pull down the shades, forget,
> Be excused from life.
> But I only covered myself with webs,
> Found only darker despair,
> A desert of quicksand —
> Tragic oblivion.

Too many young people are developing a sad and lonely detachment from life and are turning to drugs for courage, excitement, love, and some kind of fantastic miracle to fill the emptiness. When a young person jettisons all vestiges of childhood indoctrination, there is a tendency to get higher and higher, and take bigger and bigger doses in an effort to lose identity and find a newer self. The lonely drug abuser is not on a "trip to hell" nor is he practicing some kind of "holy sacrament" — he is simply seeking love and fullfillment.

5. *Loss of the Future*

It is not the "facts of life" that worry young people today but the "facts of death" hanging over their heads. We are told that the United States and Russia, between them, have stockpiled nuclear weapons — explosive power of fifteen tons of TNT for every man, woman, and child on earth. The most conservative estimates of the number of Americans who would be killed in a major nuclear attack run to about fifty million. Add to this the millions who would be blinded, maimed, burned, poisoned, and contaminated.

These facts of death are really bothering students; they consider themselves a generation without a future. Fed up with fancy clothes, fast cars, and expensive educations, many space-out on drugs as a measure of personal assurance that they will not sell out to the empty phoniness seen all around. Students now rebel at the idea of our being in competition with the Russians, the Chinese, or any other peoples. Their only question is: why can't men learn to love and understand each other and simply be a part of the human race?

POT HEADS

I used to be a traveling crusader against pot. I had a briefcase full of stories and information about how it leads to hard stuff, especially heroin. I appeared on shows with Merv Griffin, Mike Douglas, Virginia Graham, Art Linkletter, and others warning students about the dangers of blowing "smoke."

But I have been converted. Not that I think that marijuana is any less harmful than it was before — I still consider it extremely dangerous. But all the scare tactics, all the education, all the lecturing is absolutely in vain for those who have already made up their minds to turn on and groove with pot.

The great marijuana debate will continue long after all the research has ended. When the statistics are tabulated and the findings of doctors and research agencies are made public, people will still smoke pot. The horrifying anti-tobacco commercials on TV scared a lot of people, but not a single tobacco company is going out of business. Likewise, an avalanche of facts will not turn students away from pot or acid once they are committed to their course.

Those who smoke pot defend it vociferously. They know all the angles and can reel off all the arguments. They read up on the subject and become "pot conscious." They look down on anybody who speaks out against it, suggesting they are misinformed, uncool, or just too square. They choose to ignore any fact or philosophy that runs counter to their ideas about pot.

When I lectured on campus about the dangers of pot, I was swamped with all the popular arguments.

> Pot is no worse than alcohol. What about the six million adult alcoholics, the squares who are hooked on booze?
>
> Pot is just another high like a cocktail, and it's certainly not as bad as being a chain

smoker. There's no proof that it will bust your lungs.

I've tried pot and it never affected me adversely. My friends turn on, and they've never had a bad experience either.

A heavy grass trip won't waste you as much as an alcohol bender.

Pot is just a symbol of rebellion against the moral bankruptcy of parents and society.

Everybody's doing it, and soon it will be legalized — so why not enjoy it now?

Drug abusers seem to need every excuse they can find. Perhaps this explains the reason why most of the books defending the use of drugs are written by admitted drug users.

THE REAL TRUTH ABOUT POT

Pot was not invented in recent years — it is ancient. Pot was being used freely when I started working with drug users in the ghetto twelve years ago. The only thing new about pot is its widespread misuse among middle-class, educated young people and its spread into "respectable" society. As long as it was the problem of the ghettos, nobody seemed to bother. Now that pot is "in" with the sons and daughters of the affluent, well-known, and respected, everybody is sounding the alarm.

There is no doubt about it — recent polls reveal that a large percentage of the kids who are on pot today are among the most intelligent and sophisticated in their classes. There is not a single town in the country today that has not been affected. Complacent adults can quit sitting around waiting for pot to go out of style — pot is here to stay because it does exactly what youth wants it to do. It polarizes and widens every gap.

But students themselves — quite apart from the scare tactics of the adult generation — are beginning to see that pot really is a nothing path to nowhere. One student put it like this:

> "Smoking grass is really silly. You go through the ridiculous ritual of taking a toke, holding your breath, burning your throat, and getting red-eyed. You constantly worry about someone unexpectedly knocking on the door to enter the room."

I have personally worked with numbers of students addicted to pot. The experts keep telling me they are only psychologically addicted, not physiologically. But who cares about semantics? If the user can't get along without it, if it becomes a habit of the mind, he is still hooked and needs help.

Before I say another word, let me get one thing straight. I don't buy this prevalent idea that nearly every high school kid is a pot-head or that the majority of college students are acid freaks. The drug abusers may make the headlines and put parents in a state of panic, but the truth of the matter is that the majority of students will continue to reject the drug route.

Street junkies consider pot the beginning of the "route." One mainliner put it this way:

> "If a junkie is lucky, he will have a friend who will stand by him; but when the time comes only he can make the decision to stay clean.

> Even then it's never easy. Along with the
> patterns of escape your mind has developed,
> you must fight your physiological craving. I
> would be satisfied if I could turn off just one
> kid who is thinking of doing junk."

It creeps up on you. It's all fun at first — a real
groove. It could be the second joint or the two hun-
dredth — but eventually you turn on to forget some
problem, to feel good, to drift away from a situation
that bothers you. Then, friend, you are in real trouble
because you are running. You will find it easier each
time just to space-out and not face reality. It's a cop-
out! And the problems just won't go away.

Pot smokers resent the idea that they are developing "patterns of escape." But those who have gone the
whole route tell another story. Actor Joe Robinson,
who played the role of Caesar in *The Robe*, turned to
drugs at twenty-three. He lost his movie contract and
turned on with hard stuff. Now after many tragic years
he is making a great comeback. Interviewed recently,
Joey said:

> "For those who say lighter drugs aren't harm-
> ful, I say they open the door to harder drugs.
> If you've tried one, why not another one, as
> I did? Once drug use begins, you gradually
> drop out of life."

MADNESS IN MINIATURE

Few young people are now approaching pot or acid
only in a quest for pleasure or an escape — although
these are sometimes the initial reasons for involve-

ment. Most students turn to drugs with a desire to be tested by the experience. The risk involved is part of the challenge. Many of the young drug users purposely flirt with insanity. They "blow their minds," pushing themselves as close as they can to the brink of sanity without losing control. They could care less what the United States Commissioner of Narcotics has to say about drugs. The potential danger makes it groovy.

One acid head put it to me like this: "If you're messed up, dropping acid sure lets you know; but if you're a groovy person, you get a beautiful trip. You drop acid to test your head."

Asked why a sixteen-year-old would drop acid and shoot heroin, Jimmy answered:

> "You want to get stoned because it's wild, way out, strange, kind of exciting, kind of dangerous. It's just a feeling you have — you need the danger, the excitement. You need to feel it's just rotten."

THE "BANDWAGON" MADNESS CREATED BY FRIEND POWER

The Cosa Nostra cannot be blamed for drug abuse among young people anymore than a drug store can be blamed for the abuse of pills among adults. Drugs are not pushed by big organizations but by friends on campus, at parties, dances and wherever students congregate. Drugs are purchased, smuggled and sold by students who turn on their own circle of friends. Students seem to take anything and accept it as good just because "It's got to be okay if my friend gave it to me. He wouldn't give it to me if he hadn't tried it first."

Drug taking has become a communal affair, and if

the majority are "turning on," few students seem to have the moral courage to resist the herd. It may all begin with curiosity, but when the friends put on the pressure and begin to call you "square," then you have to "get with it" or be left out. Potential recruits are led to believe that everybody is turning on and, therefore, it must be groovy, cool, and safe. The biggest drug pushers in the country today are students.

Drugs, especially LSD, are not produced in sparkling laboratories by scientists in white coats but in filthy garages, in rat-infested tenement houses, and in school laboratories. Dangerous combinations are sold by students to friends anxious to "get up quick." Strychnine and rat poison have been found in doses being peddled at music festivals and on campuses.

Students who peddle drugs learn to cheat their friends worse than professional pushers cheat their customers. They sell drugs which include capsules filled with powder, sugar, or quinine. Often they peddle vitamin pills and sugar cubes impregnated with Kool-Aid. Capsules being sold in San Francisco recently were analyzed by doctors and found to contain urine with a small amount of amphetamine.

There is no quality control in the street drug trade, and unwitting student buyers are playing Russian roulette with their minds.

Student pushers deal in acid because they are convinced that it is not habit forming. They see it as an instrument in finding the true self; they even congratulate themselves that they are helping their friends to a new world of discovery. I have talked with some student acid pushers who actually had a missionary zeal.

Such publications represent the voice of the nation's drug culture. I subscribe to nearly every underground newspaper in the country, and while they plead for honest reporting and truthful debate, I have yet to find one of them which has the courage to tell the truth about drugs. They make a beautiful play on words, but when they get down to the real issue, they pour out a hodge-podge of perverted, prejudiced journalism.

I give you a classic example from the *Los Angeles Free Press:*

> The plain truth of the matter is that marijuana usage does not lead to the usage of the harder stuff. Any assertion to the contrary is a vicious flat-out lie and should be branded as such. Pot is a drug proven less harmful to humans than both alcohol and tobacco. It would be legalized but for the cigarette and liquor lobbies which are continually successful at preventing this competition.

I say that this is an outright lie and dishonest reporting. Pot has not been proven harmless to humans. Major research is underway which suggests that the opposite may be true. I can document the case histories of many heroin mainliners who would dispute every word of this whitewash by underground newspapers.

A DISEASE OF THE UNCOMMITTED

I will be accused of indiscriminately lumping acid and pot together with DMT, STP, peyote, mescaline, and the new MDA which some students are now "peaking" on. But no matter what they turn on with, it is my firm conviction that students who are committed to life and reality don't need to space-out on phony trips of escape. In twelve years of working with drug addicts, I have never met one who had a master plan for his life and a real commitment to human need. Drug abusers are always self-centered.

Tragically, many students who have already developed this pattern of escape don't see it that way. They run only with friends who use drugs. They talk about Vietnam, about prejudice, about ecology, but their talk seldom leads to involvement. They are an inward oriented group where sex behavior becomes promiscuous and ungratifying. They boast of unlimited sexual experiences, but their own sexual experiences are meaningless. They become lost souls moving from one sensuous encounter to another. They report their trips in glowing terms, but in reality their trips are empty and hollow — without significance. They are convinced they know where "it's at." The spaced-out drug user takes on a Gandhi-like attitude of passive rejection toward a world of television, draft cards, income tax, and squares. Convinced that society is insane and not worth being a part of, they drop into inner space in an effort to keep from getting up-tight.

Survival and "scoring" are the only things left of any real importance. No need of getting on top of any situation again now that "smack" has moved them into a bag of insulation. The world is seen from the bottom, filled with people who cannot help denying anyone their humanity simply because they have no idea what humanity is anymore. They have no more energy to build a better world; too weak to struggle, they seek only to survive. Actually, they don't even want to lay with each other; the only "heavy" thing is junk.

Acid freaks see the cosmos as a giant switchboard where each of our egos are like lightbulbs. By switching on certain lights and turning off others, they are convinced they can see themselves as they really want to be. When they do come down, they seem paralyzed with information and revelations they can't process and resolve. There seems to be no discharge to the wild energy which flashes through the channels of the mind triggered by acid. They become mutes who sit in corners flooding their consciousness with dream-like images. Convinced they have "plugged in" to perceptual truth, they vanish into their own network of mysticism.

More frequently now, some of those who space-out never come back. Some who have died have left handwritten letters warning of the dangers of spacing-out, while others have left frightening tape recordings. While I like to avoid any emotional aspect to narcotic abuse, I think it would pay to hear the words of eighteen-year-old Percy Pelon, Jr. who killed himself with a shotgun after spacing-out. He left a note which read:

> Where are you going to go from pot? Hash?
> Acid? Heroin? Man, if you are on the stuff,
> get off. It's never too late.

There is no such thing as a "predictable drug" — neither can there be a predictable trip. Bad drugs cause bad trips. At Woodstock, Powder Ridge, and other music festivals this warning came over the public address system: "Look out, there's a lot of bad acid around." Some obtain acid mixed with speed, two drugs which send your mind in the same direction and can push you off the deep end.

The latest trend in the drug scene is to mix narcotics and alcohol. Blues singer Janis Joplin was known to drink a quart of liquor on stage and then go to her room and shoot heroin mainline. She believed that alcohol mixed with acid or pot made for a super trip — and she paid with her life at the age of twenty-seven.

THE SATAN BUG

In the early 1960's a religious revival began to stir across the nation. Priests, ministers, and laymen were awakened to deep and dramatic experiences with God. It was the culmination of a search for an expanded consciousness and a system of true values. Students and ministers alike began to reach out for a life-changing baptism of power and love in God. Thousands of uncommitted students were caught up in this religious awakening.

Almost simultaneously with this spiritual awakening came a pseudo-religious revival through the medium of drugs. Harvard's Dr. Timothy Leary and others administered psilocybin to a group of willing seekers in a consciousness-expanding experiment in a chapel service. Out of this came a pharmacological miracle of redemption. The experiment was heralded as a total religious experience that could lead students to an understanding of God, His power and beauty, and of life beyond death.

The Christ of Calvary was no londer needed. The conventional call for holiness and sacrifice became meaningless. Now you could just drop a sugar cube and be baptized. You could space-out on a pill and see God. You could short-cut the Biblical route to Jesus and "get right to the Holy Ghost" — as one student told me.

While God was pouring out the Holy Spirit baptism, Satan began pouring out the unholy spirit baptism. I am personally convinced that the psychedelic revolution was demonically inspired to negate the genuine ministry of the Holy Spirit.

Divinity students who returned from acid trips gave glowing accounts of visions of God, and revelations of Christ — visions of hell, of sin and evil self. This attempt to defuse the outpouring of the Holy Spirit has failed. Today, as never before, sons and daughters are receiving the Holy Spirit and in that experience finding reality.

Timothy Leary ended up in custody of the Black Panthers in Algeria, and many of his followers have turned to Satan worship. Visions of God have turned to visions of demons and indescribable evil images.

Students who have bent their minds on acid and opened themselves up to mystical experiences through drugs will never go back to dead churches which offer only shallow religion. They are ready now for the deep things of the Holy Spirit. They must find — and find it quick — an experience that far surpasses every past drug trip. It must be real — heart-searching — ego-smashing — different and dramatic. The baptism in the Holy Spirit offers all this and more.

If the church fails to challenge these newly opened minds, they may turn to Eastern cults or devil worship and be lost forever to Christ's message.

I have yet to find a Satan worshiper who did not first open his mind to mystical experiences through drugs. Devil worshipers are graduates of the school of psychedelia.

6

Coming Apart

Coming Apart

A SCRIPTURAL REBUKE FOR
PROBLEM PUSHERS

A young divorcé went to his mother-in-law's house to visit his family. His ex-wife was gone, and he asked to see his six-month-old son. Fifteen minutes later the wife arrived to find him sitting in the baby's room in a trance. Running to an open window, she discovered the child's dead body lying on the pavement below. All he could answer was: "I just had to do it. Something made me. I couldn't help myself. I just came apart."

The mayor of New York City was forced to make a special television appearance to tell of his alarm at the rash of child beatings. A four-year-old girl was found floating in the East River. The father admitted that he had beaten her to death, thrown her in the river, and reported her missing. Later he confessed, "I just couldn't stop. I couldn't help myself. Everything fell apart."

A sixteen-year-old drug abuser sat in my office crying out her tragic story. She had been brought to my office by a Christian brother who had almost killed her accidentally the previous night. Dashing in front of his car, she had made a stomping motion as if to trample his car underfoot. Slamming on the brakes, he rushed to her aid and found her to be high on acid. The gentleman and his wife kept her overnight and in the morning brought her to me. I learned she had tripped out on acid about fifty times and had become so scrambled in her mind that she had dropped out of school. (Ironically, she had been in my daughter's class.) High on acid, she saw the trees come to life, the sidewalks swelled like ocean waves, colors danced everywhere, people took on strange and confused images, and cars looked like tiny ants. Stepping into the flow of traffic, she attempted to "stomp the ants" to death. She was nearly killed in the process.

Debbie's story is like that of so many other teenagers today who confess they are "coming apart." Six months prior to this time she had never even touched a cigarette, let alone pot, pills, or acid. One day a well-mannered boy entered the pizza parlor where she and her friends were. He had five joints of pot and was looking for a few others who wanted to drag with him. She had heard so much about pot — everybody in school had been discussing the pros and cons of drug use — she decided to experiment and see for herself.

The first stick of pot hit her right and she remembered it as "a very beautiful experience, peaceful and relaxing." A week later she was dragging on five and six joints at a time. Her first acid trip came a few weeks later.

Now, after about fifty trips on acid, she sat trembling in my office, trying to explain her deepest emotions.

> "I have a sense of losing my mind. It seems to be fragmenting into a million pieces and floating out into space. I try to reach out and put them back together, but I can't reach the pieces — they float away so fast. I'm coming apart. Death seems to me like a beautiful trip — a place where my mind can be put back together again."

Debbie refused my help, insisting there was nothing wrong in hanging around with old friends who turned her on. Somewhere, even now, she is still watching her mind fall to pieces.

The average daily newspaper today reads as though it were being published in hell. Tragic and horrible things happen so frequently that we get hardened to it all and turn to the comics or sports pages. In one recent paper I found the following stories:

"RED DEVILS" TAKE OVER HIGH SCHOOL

The Wainnae High School in Honolulu was disrupted by up to 200 students under the influence of "red devil" barbituates. Principal Milton Shishido said, "I haven't heard of anything ever on a scale this large. Most of the students were dazed and wandering around campus. Some of them could hardly walk. It was frightening." The principal said over 2,000 pills were sold or given away free by a number of unknown pushers when buses arrived at school. Two hours later, classes had to be suspended because of brawling and the condition of drugged students. It has been called the worst case of mass drug abuse in Hawaiian history. Teachers saw kids jumping into fountains; others fell asleep in class.

CANNIBALISM IN MONTANA

The body of James M. Schlossen, a missing Montana social worker, was found at a Yellowstone River campsite. The body was armless, legless, headless, and the heart was missing. Stanley Baker, 22, and Harvey Stroup were arrested; each of the young men was carrying a human finger bone. One of them admitted to police: "I have a problem; I am a cannibal." Baker told them he had eaten Schlossen's heart. Baker belonged to a cult that used drugs.

NINE-YEAR-OLD BOY FOUND DRUGGED

A nine-year-old boy was found on a drug induced trip-out in the middle of traffic in San Jose. The boy was trying to stop cars at a busy intersection by waving his hands. The lad said someone "gave him a pill." He told police officers, "Everything is moving, changing, growing." He was rushed to Valley Medical Center, where it was confirmed he was hallucinating on some kind of drug.

SOLDIERS IN VIETNAM TURN TO DRUGS

The Navy is alarmed over increased use of marijuana and LSD by the armed forces. Marijuana is just as available in Vietnam as chewing gum is in the United States. Master Chief Marvin Reed, who spent a year in Vietnam as a drug abuse lecturer, said:

> "All one has to do is go to a fence and throw a dollar bill over and a ten pack of M will come sailing back."

In this same newspaper appeared stories of wars, rumors of wars, rape, nudity, suicide, strikes, violence, campus unrest, murder of all kinds, and ads for a dozen dirty, X-rated movies.

What strange and terrible thing is happening to this generation? What unseen power is causing things to come apart so quickly? What is it that drives thousands of teen-agers out of their homes and into the lonely streets? Why do normal teen-agers suddenly turn to drugs and violence? Why do we have more homosexuals? More mass murders? More sex crimes? More filth and corruption than ever in history?

AN ARMY OF SEDUCERS

Seducing spirits are loose on the earth. False teachers and evil men are getting worse and worse. The Bible warns: "But wicked men and imposters will go on from bad to worse, deceiving and being deceived" (II Timothy 3:13). The Bible describes an impostor or false teacher as one who:

> walks in the flesh,
> wallows in lust and uncleanness,
> despises the government,
> is presumptuous and self-willed, proud,
> speaks evil of dignitaries and leaders,
> riots against things he cannot comprehend,
> has eyes full of sex and adultery,
> goes about duping unstable people,
> speaks swelling words of vanity and violence,
> promises freedom while all the time he is bound,
> vomits out corruption and, like a dog,
> wallows in his own filth. (II Peter 2)

These impostors and seducers have lost faith in God, in their country and flag, in their parents, and in all of society. They demand freedom to use drugs, to engage in perversion, and to live with no restrictions. They look to Che Guevara as a savior, to Mao as a modern God, and to Castro as a redeemer. Cops are called "pigs"; the flag is spit upon and used as a rag; the President is called a fascist; Christ is considered a dead symbol of the establishment church.

SHALL WE ALL GO HIDE IN A CAVE?

Elijah, the prophet, already tried that — and it didn't work. This great man of God saw his generation coming apart and decided to just "hold out to the end."

> When he arrived there, he lodged in a cave. Presently the word of the Lord came to him: What are you doing here, Elijah? (I Kings 19:9)

Get this picture firmly in your mind: a great man of God hiding out in a cave, disillusioned, full of fear, developing ulcers, and ready to throw in the sponge. Elijah gave up on his generation. He simply quit and went into hiding.

But God would have no servant of His hiding from these overwhelming odds. God asked: "What are you doing in this dark cave, Elijah?"

The prophet's answer has a familiar ring to it. Paraphrased, he was saying to God:

> I have been a conservative, hard-working minister. But the nation is coming apart. Ahab's government is the most corrupt in history. The church has disintegrated, and false prophets have defiled the altars. The earth is filled with violence; a sword is in the land. It is a sinful people, laden with iniquities, a seed of evildoers, children who are corrupters. Revolt

has stricken the heart. The cities are burned with fire, and strangers devour the land. From the sole of the feet even to the head there is no soundness in the land — but bruises, wounds, putrifying sores.

After Elijah cried out his despair and hopelessness, God asked again: "But why are you hiding in this cave?" It was almost too much for this devoted, hard-working prophet. Listen to his heartrending answer:

I am in this cave because everybody else has forsaken Your law; everybody else has picked up the sword, slain the prophets, and thrown down Your altars. And I only am left. They got to everybody but me.

ARE THINGS REALLY AS BAD AS THEY SEEM?

The prophet had become so conscious of the many things that appeared to be coming apart that he was blind to the tremendous underground movement which had been developing.

And the Lord said to him: Go back . . . . I still have left 7,000 in the land who have not bowed down and kissed the idols of Baal . . . . Anoint young Hazael to be king over Syria. Go, anoint Jehu to be king over Israel. Go, anoint the young prophet Elisha to take up your mantle . . . .

The lesson is clear. Things appear to be hopeless. Things appear to be coming apart. But it is no time to hide. In times like these, great spiritual revolutions are born. Yes, the land is troubled, sin is rampant, and gross darkness covers the earth, but God is still King of the flood.

There is an army of youth who have not bowed to the false idols of today. Young, fiery revolutionaries are even now being raised up in our midst who will turn the tide. Young men and women of faith, un-hampered by materialistic hang-ups, will stand up to help purge the land and bring in a new day. Sons and daughters will prophesy. The Spirit will anoint this generation as none in past history.

What a glorious day to be alive! What a great day of opportunity this is! Let's get out of our caves. Let's express a new confidence in the young generation. There are more Jehus and Elishas among them.

Prophets of doom have created a panic in this nation. If I am to believe all I read and hear in the news media, I would have to believe that every American teen-ager is a pot-head and all college kids are acid freaks toting guns and taking over campuses. That simply is not true. The majority of our youth are still square — still clean and down on all drugs.

The church of Christ has not failed. Parents are not all failures either. Society is not all bad. Government is not always corrupt. Let's quit being problem pushers and renew our faith in God — and in His children.

Paul, the apostle, reminds us:

> Do you not know what the Scripture says concerning Elijah? . . . I have kept for Myself seven thousand men who have not bowed the knee to Baal. Just so there is at present a remnant in accordance with His gracious choice. (Romans 11:2-5)

THIS IS NOT A WHITEWASH

I see the problems. I have been working in gutters and ghettos too long to be visionary. It is true that drug addiction now touches the lives of pre-teeners in nearly every suburb. Younger kids are getting hooked. Movies and books are dirty. Violence and lawlessness abound. But there is also a trend in the other direction.

Clean-up crusades are underway in high schools throughout the country. An attempt is being made to rat on the pushers and isolate the abusers. Hippie types are beginning to come all the way back. Acid rock has given way to a new sound. Meditation is replacing acid and speed on college campuses.

I beg every establishment cave dweller to arise — Go! Anoint the young. There is a new generation ready to put it all together. With Paul, say with confidence, "Just so there is at present a remnant . . . ."

7 Ditching

 Ditching

REACHING RUNAWAYS

Here come the "ditchers," rolling stones hoping to "find themselves" on the road. They are the more than one million kids who run away from home each year. Among them are the youth culturists, the hip tribalists, the drug freaks, the under-thirtys who reject society, and the "easy rider" just looking for thrills.

In the 1950s and 60s the mystics and floaters who thumbed rides were called "hitchers." A ditcher differs in that running away has become a way of life. You simply ditch school, parents, church, obligations, old friends, and offer your thumb as a ticket to a new way of life.

Today runaways can virtually disappear in the underground community in any major city. They are constantly reassured by the growing number of young people doing the same thing and feel safe in their numbers.

It has never been easier to ditch than it is today. The ditcher can get free medical attention at clinics, free room and board with "brothers and sisters" who sell underground papers, and "split" successfully from home in just a few days.

"Leaving Home for Fun and Profit" is a two-page compendium on running away. It was first published in Washington's "Quicksilver Times," and it tells how to "scare the life" out of parents back home. It tells how to obtain fake identification, credit cards, driver's license, bogus social security and Selective Service cards, and even how to get hold of a fake birth certificate. It relates how to dye hair, change appearances, shoplift, and how to survive like an undercover agent in a foreign land. There is even a suggestion on how to arrange for a set of "on call" parents, a willing couple who will handle police calls and references.

WHY DO KIDS DITCH?

Recent studies suggest the ditchers are not predominantly products of broken homes or problem environments; rather, they are ordinary young people much like the straights who stay at home. Some ditch because parents are too strict or too unconcerned; others ditch because of quarreling with parents over long hair and unconventional styles. I've even encountered kids who ditched simply because dad and mom made them come in before midnight.

I met five innocent-looking, teen-age girls in East Village, New York. Four were only thirteen and one was fourteen years old. They had ditched from suburban homes in a small town in New Jersey and had been living for two weeks in an abandoned, burnt-out apartment house on 3rd Street. They slept on burlap sacks and panhandled for food. Dirty, uncombed, hungry, and pimply faced — they seemed to me as though they were ready to go back to the straight life at home. But at TEEN CHALLENGE we never "rat" on kids who run away, and we do not force them to return home — simply because they will run away again in a few weeks if they are forced to return.

Sandy, the oldest, spoke for the group. They had read my book *The Cross and the Switchblade* and believed they could trust me. She began:

> "Mr. Wilkerson, we ditched all at the same time and for the same reasons. You've probably heard that kids run away because of phony parents, phony society, the war, etc. Maybe a few — but most ditchers are like us. It's very simple. We got tired of doing dishes, tired of doing schoolwork, tired of being told what we could do and where we could go — so we ditched. To tell you the truth — we're all just a little bit lazy.

Sandy and her friends had been gone for over two weeks; their parents had no idea where they were. None of them were "down" on their parents; rather, they all admitted their parents were good and they felt mutual love and respect. They simply wanted to do their own thing, smoke pot, drop some acid, investigate life, and get away from all responsibility. Not one would give me permission to call home and let their parents know they had not been raped or kidnapped and were still alive. Hungry, lonely, sick, dirty, just floating around — they said they were happy with their way of life. They would not go home — would not change for anybody.

DITCHING "APOSTLES"

In California, and now coast to coast, you see the ditchers traveling here and there like restless spirits seeking a place to land. I stopped to question a fourteen-year-old girl hitchhiking near an entrance to the San Diego Freeway.

"How do you know which car to get in? Can you be sure you won't be molested or attacked? Aren't you afraid to ride along with just anyone? Why are you carrying a Bible?"

She smiled and said,

> "The Bible is for real — I'm a Jesus person. I've asked the Lord to bless me while I'm ditching. I'm sort of a missionary, and I hitch a ride just to talk to people. I have no place I call home — just anywhere is okay. As for getting in the wrong car, I've worked out sort of a little plan. For example anybody who drives a VW is all right. Also, anyone who has a peace sign in the window won't hurt you. I know I'm safe in those psychedelic vans and flower cars. I try not to ride with

older, white men — they're dangerous. I know what I'm doing could be dangerous, but so far God has protected me. I like being full-time for Jesus."

She is only one of a growing army of ditching "apostles" who are convinced that reality can be found only in literally "forsaking" father, mother, houses, lands, and friends for the Gospel's sake. They have established communes, training centers, monasteries, and farms where Bible study is the only pursuit and "bugging" the establishment is the only goal. They interpret the Bible literally and believe only absolute rejection of home and family can result in a spiritual revolution. Some of these groups now attract a large following, mostly from the drug culture. The publicity they receive does not reveal their true identity or their doctrinaire. Teen-agers seeking the deeper things of Christ are easily led into this way of life. There are plenty of Scriptures, when taken out of context, that support the ditching philosophy of some of the new Jesus movements.

I know of one ditching organization, made up entirely of former drug users, who travel the nation crying out against organized religion — and who always leave town with a new supply of converts. Alarmed parents have contacted me to help them get a son or daughter away from some group of ditchers who "brainwashed" the child into running away without leaving word of their departure. Weeks later things were discovered missing from the house, and it was learned the leaders of the group encouraged stealing from parents to support the group. The Scripture basis for such stealing — "all things are yours . . . ."

The reasons kids ditch are becoming more visible with each passing day — and it's time to hear these reasons and take them to heart:

"I just left because I had to. I'm crashing, and I know where it will all end. But why? It's a crazy something that hits you and holds you and you can't explain or justify it — you just go."

"My mother wanted me to get rid of my dog. She said if I loved her, I'd do it. I loved my dog, too, and she made me choose. My dog was always there and she wasn't — so I went out to the streets with my dog."

"When my parents discovered I had experimented with drugs, they told me I was a bad influence on my little brother and sister — so I had to get out. They figured it was a solution to keep them safe. Me? They would sacrifice me for them. I guess now I would have been a drug user anyhow — even if they let me stay."

"Mom gave up on me because she said I couldn't be handled. We argued all the time. She just threw up her hands and told me I was hopeless. I said, Who needs this — so I split."

"I'm not running away from anything. I guess I'm trying to run to something. I think my parents were really the ones who were running away. I'm just looking for something better than they had. My parents were completely miserable. I knew leaving home could not be any worse."

"I ran off to my first rock festival and kept on going. My parents can have all the glory, all the money — give me freedom. I fill up my days by visiting the library, visiting friends, learning all about drugs, and doing new things. I get sick a lot, and it gets pretty cold and lonely sometimes — but someday I'll really be free."

"I just wanted to get away from everybody's hang-ups. I don't want to change the world, just myself. Maybe I'm looking for a new set of rules for my life; the old ones didn't work."

"Dropping-out is a transitory stage. When I first split a few years ago, everything was violent and political. Now, things are getting serious. I'm going back, and I think a lot of kids are going back. But it's going to be very difficult. We will be separated in a different way. It will not be a physical gap anymore. We'll go home, and parents will be glad. But we will still be worlds apart. It will be a spirit gap. We will overpower their emotions and spirits. We will go back because nothing works by separating from the power sources."

WE NEED TO LEARN FROM THE DITCHERS

Through all of this I get a message — loud and clear. Young people would rather not ditch; they do so hoping things will change and everything will somehow work out. But they do not want to return to a world of meaningless Sunday schools, dead Masses, empty liturgies, and phony religious put-ons.

The truth is, Jesus people who are now forsaking a life of drugs and violence are turning in great numbers to the churches and to the men of God who practice a simple form of worship and who offer no-foolishness kind of programs. They are gathering in small groups to study the Bible, hoping to find the key to overcoming the pressures of this complex age. They refuse to support fancy church buildings with unnecessary "gingerbread" — giving instead to feed the poor and minister to the derelicts of society.

These ditchers who have returned and who now seek the path of true values have much to teach the man or woman of God who seeks to understand and reach the runaways of this generation. Some of the things they say are true — and it hurts. The lessons they have learned are invaluable.

1. *The neon god of materialism
   is corrupting humanity.*

Some of the ditchers tell the story of the Cadillac that drove up to the Plaza Hotel. The chauffeur helped the mother out—then the twenty-six pieces of matched luggage. The son who had been sitting in the back of the car was placed in a wheelchair. As he was being wheeled into the hotel, the manager murmured a few discreet words of sympathy to the mother.

"Why, what's wrong?" she demanded.

"Your son, not being able to walk," he said.

"Of course he can walk. Thank God, he doesn't have to."

Today's kids have been so baptized in "things" they have developed marshmallow philosophies. Seldom needing to make choices or decisions, they learn to postpone things. They have learned how to enjoy the pleasures heaped upon them by doting parents but have not been taught to cope with pain. There is no challenge to develop a will, so they are often easily led by rebels and drug abusers. "Instamatic" family atmosphere has tired both generations and left everyone bewildered that so much wealth could cause so much misery.

I met a wealthy businessman recently who told me his children made him sell a "very long, special-made" Cadillac. It featured a built-in TV, bar, telephone, and leather top. They would not ride in it and insisted it be sold so they could face their friends. This millionaire was secretly delighted that his two teen-agers were so uncomfortable with material things. He was, in fact, rather relieved by their preference for the simple way of life. His kids did not want a big allowance and refused to live in a palatial mansion in Beverly Hills. The family moved into a smaller residence.

This father is learning something we must all learn about the majority of youth today. They are totally "fed up" with materialism. They refuse to equate success with big cars, bank accounts, and mountains of things. They see materialism as the seed of corruption and so they ditch it all to be free from its power.

Who really needs help? Parents who are caught up in the mad race for bigger houses, swimming pools, deep freezes, Cadillacs, and prestige positions — or the kid who sits alone, cold and lonely, in a city park without a penny to his name, trying to understand why God put him on this planet?

Who really needs a sermon? The minister who schemes and dreams of bigger pensions, bigger churches, bigger budgets, bigger staff — or the runaway girl who left the church — ditched it all — because she felt lost in the crowd, convinced no one in the pulpit or pew really cared enough to listen personally to her deep emotional needs?

Perhaps some of us, as parents and ministers, should shake off the chains of security and affluence and march with a sign reading, "Down with materialism — Down with the love of ease — Down with the love of money!"

2. The church is dead because it really doesn't believe in miracles any longer.

One ditcher described the church as "a mausoleum where dead saints haunt the living." I have never been one to criticize the church, and I'm still convinced many ministers today are godly men who weep over the needs of lost humanity, but these kids are not leaving the church for phony reasons. Teen-agers are not anti-God, anti-Christ, or anti-religious. They simply refuse to playact at faith like so many of their parents. They refuse to go through empty formalities and sit through an uncomfortable hour watching a "doubting Thomas" put on some liturgical act. They are fed up with political parsons who seem more interested in relevance than repentance.

This is a generation of seekers, and the majority are seeking answers from the Bible. They read that it is possible to have access to the Heavenly Father — that it is possible to boldly enter God's presence — that it is possible to get prayers answered — that is is possible by faith to overcome all their obstacles — and they are no longer willing to listen to the double-talk of some seminary graduate who tries to tell them "it may not necessarily be so."

THE REVOLUTION IS ON

Hear me loud and clear! This ditching generation is ready to hear the language of faith. They are ready to believe for miracles. It is a reaching, hungering generation ready to come alive and see visions.

I predict we will soon witness the greatest spiritual revolution of all times. Young men and women are going to walk this land and cry out for the Spirit. God will take the foolish of the world — the weak addict, the ditchers, the converted hippies and prostitutes — and confound the wise. While influential church leaders involve themselves in politics and church union, they will be stealing the headlines and the Holy Ghost thunder. Churches will spring up on beaches — in living rooms — in barns — in open fields — in brush arbors — in school corridors — in coffee houses — and they will be the true army the prophet Joel saw coming to birth.

Young people will be preaching Jesus at music festivals, in school assemblies, on the street, in prisons, at home, and any place where more than two or three are gathered. Ministers who are walking in the Spirit, who will open their doors to them, who will try to understand them, and who will patiently guide and teach them will reap a great harvest.

Ministers who denounce them, who refuse to trust them, who allow past prejudices to influence them, and who refuse to change will be left with nothing but their memories of "how it used to be."

As much as any minister living today, I want to help reach this generation. I long to see them sanctified and living holy lives. I want to hold on to the principles of God's holy Word that are unchangeable — but I have jettisoned my narrow-mindedness, my pig-headedness, my loveless doctrines, my dogmatic methods, my cocky attitudes, and my cute criticisms.

Instead, I hope to engage in a day-by-day ministry of understanding and a willingness to change as compassion demands it. I will not be moved from Christ — His call for holiness and the crucified and resurrected life. But I am going to change as a man, as a minister. I am going to get my hands off any throat — and reach out to lift and love.

Student War on Drug Abuse

Appendix: Student War on Drug Abuse

MY NEW MESSAGE TO YOUNG
PEOPLE ABOUT DRUG ABUSE

Everybody is screaming about the "alarming increase" in drug abuse, but nobody seems to want to talk about the "encouraging interest" the majority of students are showing in combatting drug abuse. Students are resisting the bandwagon philosophy and a new message is now heard: "The only students who use are those who need it."

I say it's time to declare war on drug abuse, and this battle can be won only by the students themselves. All the experts, the ministers, the agencies, the do-gooders, the parents — all are really helpless unless students take drastic steps to change their own world. We need students who are not afraid to bring the "space-outs" back to earth.

"What can one student do to combat drug abuse?" I can think of a number of practical things that I believe will really work.

1. *Convince yourself and your friends that drugs are physically harmful to the body.*

All short-term psychic benefits are gained at a terrible price. Drugs cost in physical well-being and self-reliance, and the long-range effect on the human body is disastrous. Weigh the benefits of using drugs against the proven losses. Take a good look around you at all the individuals who have been using drugs for a long period of time and see how much they have lost. They started by saying they were not using drugs as an escape or a crutch, but now they have made drugs an end in themselves. No high is worth it if it costs you clarity of mind.

Deep-freeze your convictions about narcotic use. Don't become prejudiced for or against drugs — just look at the facts and be honest with yourself. You shall know the truth and the truth shall set you free. One student who stands up against the use of drugs can save ten others who are on the fence.

2. *Don't be seduced by the "art of letting go."*

The idea of "letting go" or "turning on" has been romanticized as the ultimate experience. The way of excess is supposed to lead to the palace of wisdom. Madness scares young people — yet schizophrenic breakdowns only seem to seduce more young people to sink into the dark, deep waters.

"Turning on" has a dangerous, alluring sound, almost like "the art of loving."

There is absolutely nothing romantic about living on the thin edge — between sanity and madness, childhood and adulthood, love and hate. The mind is not a "truth lab" in which to experiment.

The concept of challenge is alien to most turned-on students because they seek only to experience. They reach for some light and understanding in a superficial way.

Turned-on students usually want to talk with no one except fellow trippers who have become part of a secret brotherhood. Dropping acid becomes a sort of anesthetic used to blast out the "games" of square society.

Two ways of life are now clearly visible, side by side, and too many students are tossing from one to the other. There is a wild call to "split" from the middle-class status race and choose an alternate way of life. A wealthy man in the construction business joins a commune and drops out of sight. A college professor walks out of the classroom, gets on his cycle, and heads for the hills.

Each in his own way is trying to turn on and escape from the net which binds him to tradition. This "easy rider" philosophy sounds good on paper but in actuality leads to an existence crowded with more hang-ups than were present before the new-found freedom. No wonder turned-on people have to stay stoned — they are desperately trying to escape from their escape.

3. *Stay on top of life.*

Something may be missing in your life; perhaps you don't have the vaguest notion what it is. However, if you want to shift direction and become a self-examiner or answer-seeker, don't let your mind get out of control with drugs — you'll be on the wrong track. These drugs are not called "mind benders" for nothing. You can block off your growth and cut off your senses by using drugs to get rid of your hang-ups.

You cannot stay on top of life if you lose your sense of wholeness. The entire socio-political structure may somehow be out of control, and perhaps there may be no remedy — all the more reason to keep from blowing your own mind.

You may deplore the idea of becoming a success, but there is nothing wrong with understanding and enjoying the process by which you succeed honestly. You don't have to struggle to become rich and famous, but you can employ a process by which you obtain wealth to give to those who are in need. You don't have to become a Wall Street broker or a society doctor, but you can be involved in the process of discipline and diligence necessary to reach these goals.

Most important of all, remember that the need which causes you to experiment with drugs is the same need which may keep you going back until you are hooked. I don't care if everybody around you is turning on, there is power available to insulate yourself against drug abuse.

4. *Join the Jesus revolution.*

Maybe you haven't heard yet, but there is a Jesus revolution all over the world. *Look Magazine* recently described this movement.

A crusade — a massive, fundamentalist, Christ-as-personal-Savior revival — has caught hold in California, and it shows every sign of sweeping East and becoming a national preoccupation. It's an old-time, Bible-toting, witness-giving kind of revival, and the new evangelists are the young.

Who are these Jesus people? They are the thousands of students, poor and middle class — many formerly spaced-out, junkies, and rebels — who are finding truth and revelation in the person of Jesus Christ.

Holy Spirit vibrations are being felt across the nation. The Spirit is revealing to students the truth that is in Jesus — and those who find this truth have ended their search. They no longer need to turn on. Thousands who have been messed up by "smack" have been made clean by His power.

It is not a false, mass-produced, Hollywood-directed kind of spiritual awakening — but something deep and personal. This spiritual awakening has touched communes in nearly every state. Students from Protestant, Catholic, and Jewish backgrounds are finding a common bond in the love of Christ.

Speaking of one commune, a reporter said, "Most inhabitants were on some form of dope. Now they are blowing their minds on Jesus, and it's a positive high. They're high, and they're smiling that unquestioning, knowing smile that seems a symptom, a symbol, of the Jesus movement."

There is a world to change; this is the greatest day of opportunity in all of history. While some may be flirting with the thought of turning on and spacing out with drugs, others are leaving the drug scene completely and are now spending their time helping those who are addicted.

Christ offers courage to face the crowd. He can take any weak-willed student and turn him into a fully committed person who has the power and courage to stand up and be counted. He also gives the individual the respect of the crowd for being different.

Soon you must cross a line. You have to decide once and for all which way you will go. Some of you, having read this book, will still turn on and drop out. Nothing I have said will change your minds because you are convinced I am wrong and that you are different and can make it with drugs. But I believe the majority of students will stay on the side of sanity.

Jesus Christ promises in His Word to keep your mind in perfect peace if you keep it focused on Him. Open every window and door of your heart, and you can not only expand your consciousness but you can become an entirely new person in Him. Old things will pass away; all things will become new.

The Jesus revolution has begun. The Jesus people are coming. Join! Become a Jesus person yourself and discover the meaning of reality.